Woman

Kaz Riley
BSc. PDCHyp CHyp BSCH

Praise for Woman

Kaz's book guides you step by step into recovering your natural ease and acceptance - appreciation even - of your sexuality as a woman. She walks you through ideas, permission to experience joy and desire, information you'll need to know, and actual exercises to get you started. A great resource for women wanting an overview and solid starting place. Thank you for writing this, Kaz!

DR. BETTY MARTIN
Developer of the *Wheel of Consent*, wheelofconsentbook.com

Kaz offers a brilliant and thorough discussion of female sexuality - what it is, and why we don't know what we don't know.

Woman is a well-researched and medically accurate explanation of why, and how, women struggle with sensuality and pleasure. This book empowers women to honor their bodies and own their pleasure. Kaz's exercises will take the reader on a scenic journey from "How did we get here?" to "What do I actually feel and believe about my sexuality?" to "How I can get the sexual relationship with myself I want." The reader will enjoy the trip!

Woman teaches the reader to connect to her body and her erotic self, fully and without guilt or shame. It is essentially the instruction manual that should come with the female body to show how to access the intense pleasure the mind-body is designed to give her. I can't wait to recommend *Woman* to my sex therapy clients... and, when she reaches adolescence, I will gift it to my daughter! It's that good!

MeLanie Modjoros, MD
AASECT Certified Sexuality Counselor

If you are a woman or love women, I would consider this book essential reading.

Kaz has created a comprehensive and accurate guide which flies in the face of centuries of harmful, damaging and inaccurate narratives about the mysteries of female sexuality. The truth is that our capacity is far greater and more magnificent than most of us have ever dared to dream, and this book, through Kaz's genius, manages to lay it out in an organised easy to understand way that would be helpful to anyone. Do yourself or the women in your life a favour and read it. Your life will never be the same. I expect Kaz to enter the category of Great Women who have changed the sexual landscape for women, clearing and paving and guiding the path to sexual freedom.

Freja Njorden
The Sensualist Podcast

This is undoubtedly a book that will be talked about for years to come. This will change minds, change relationships and change lives. Educational, inspirational, challenging, practical and fun – Kaz Riley somehow gets the balance exactly right. My frequent response when reading and re-reading this book was, "Why has no one written this before?" As a fellow therapist and author, I do not say this lightly, but I have no doubt that we have an instant classic on our hands. I will certainly be buying copies for my clients, friends, family and partners. This book truly is a gift to be treasured.

Graham Old
Solution-focused therapist, certified hypnotist and author

Kaz has a gift for gently exposing the oppressive lie that women should be ashamed or embarrassed of their sexuality then guiding the reader through the exact, enjoyable process of reclaiming and unveiling her innate sensuality in a way that enriches every area of life. Thank you Kaz for bringing this much needed message to the world.

LORI HAMMOND
Silence the Imposter Monster Podcast

A refreshing perspective on sex and sexuality. As a licensed marriage and family therapist, I will find the ideas Kaz put forth as useful guides for helping my clients. I love the author's wit and fresh perspectives, but even more, I love the practical applications and the Embrace Techniques that are actionable strategies for developing mindful sex.

DR. RICHARD NONGARD
LMFT

Kudos to Kaz Riley!

Kaz Riley is the established expert in the field of hypnosis for sexual empowerment and it shows. Her long-awaited book, Woman—How to Find, Understand, and Embrace Your Sexual Pleasure, is finally here—and I cannot give it a high enough commendation. Filled with insights, examples, and plenty of helpful exercises, Kaz's wonderful book helps open hearts, minds, and, well, vaginas, to an ecstasy we may never have known, or perhaps ever realised we desire.

Throughout the pages of *Woman*, Kaz skillfully and sensitively addresses a topic that is so often conveyed as shameful—if it is even conveyed at all—that many people will barely let themselves think about it, let alone utter words like sex, sexual pleasure, orgasm. Kaz does just that, however—she talks about it all. Vociferously. Kaz doesn't shy away from this subject, she knows how essential it is to address it, to give it presence, to understand it, and to live it.

For far too long women have been objectified, criticised, and judged, dismissed and discounted, bullied and shamed. By men, yes, but sadly by women as well. We are regularly assessed by our looks, and especially by body shape and weight and size. Men can strut around half naked, huge harry bellies spilling over their pants, oblivious; women, on the other hand, dress to disguise their "flaws", deprive themselves constantly, make love with the lights off. Not in every case, but this is quite common.

The concept of sexual pleasure does not exist in a vacuum. We can deepen our understandings about sex and pleasure, we can learn techniques designed to create and stimulate, but ultimately feeling uncomfortable or insecure about our bodies is not conducive to sexual pleasure, regardless of anything else we might employ. Kaz speaks to that too. Her book is powerful and unprecedented, and we are greatly blessed to have access to its wisdom.

As Divine Feminine reclaims her rightful place in this world, so shall we honor Her in recognising our own Goddess selves, owning our needs and our feelings, and accepting—truly appreciating—the glorious, tangible bodies so graciously housing our essence. And so shall we embrace ourselves as Woman, fully and completely, no longer whispering but shouting – with Kaz guiding the way!

Lynsi Eastburn, MA
HypnoFertility Creator and Specialist
Author of *The 3 Keys to Conception* and other books on the topic.

When I first met Kaz in person some years back, I told my wife Lynsi, "This is a woman who will be doing things." Lynsi said the same thing and the work that Kaz has been doing has only served to prove us right. I realise that this book is focused on female sexuality, but as a man, I found a great deal of value in these pages and perhaps this will inspire Kaz to write a male edition, or perhaps a version that all sexes can enjoy together. I consider myself to have been lucky to deal with many sexual issues in my own practice. At one time the town of Trinidad here in my state of Colorado was the sex change capital of the world, and I was privileged to work with a large number of those individuals and help them along their journey. I have also been lucky enough to work with individuals who identified as male but did not possess a Y chromosome and I have worked with those who possessed a Y chromosome and identified as female. It is time we embrace the many variations of sexuality and treat everyone with dignity and respect.

I am impressed with how well thought out, professionally written, and in depth this book is. There is a plethora of information within, and I think readers will find the exercises to be very helpful. Our sexuality is something that would seem to be natural, but people have little understanding of it, and far too often, many fears about it. This book will increase that understanding along with the good work Ms Riley performs on a daily basis. I wholeheartedly recommend this book.

Drake Eastburn, BCH, CI
Author of *The Therapeutic Hypnotist,*
What is Hypnosis (Really)? and several others.

Woman

How to Find, Understand and Embrace Your Sexual Pleasure

Kaz Riley

BSc. PDCHyp CHyp BSCH

Purple Pendant
L T D

Woman

How to Find, Understand and Embrace Your Sexual Pleasure

Cover Design by: Nskvsky

Edited by: Lauren Butler

Photography: John Steel Photography

ISBN: 978-1-9196090-0-3

DISCLAIMER: The publisher and the author are providing this book and its contents on an "as is" basis and make no representations or warranties of any kind with respect to this book or its contents. The publisher and the author disclaim all such representations and warranties, including but not limited to warranties of healthcare for a particular purpose. In addition, the publisher and the author assume no responsibility for errors, inaccuracies, omissions, or any other inconsistencies herein.

The content of this book is for informational purposes only and is not intended to diagnose, treat, cure, or prevent any condition or disease. You understand that this book is not intended as a substitute for consultation with a licensed practitioner. Please consult with your own physician or healthcare specialist regarding the suggestions and recommendations made in this book. The use of this book implies your acceptance of this disclaimer.

The publisher and the author make no guarantees concerning the level of success you may experience by following the advice and strategies contained in this book, and you accept the risk that results will differ for each individual.

Dedication

I dedicate this book to my wonderful clients and students;
you are my inspiration.

Acknowledgements

There are many amazing people that have supported and inspired me throughout my career and the process of writing this book. Special thanks to my mentors, motivators and cheerleading team, Lynsi Eastburn, Greg Beckett, Kelley Woods, Karen Hand, Freja Njorden, Shelly Stockwell, Stephanie Conkle, Maria Bird, Gila Zak, Heather Spalding, Imaginatrix, Alexandrea Riley and Eileen Riley. Thank you to Dr. Richard Nongard for his guidance and structure throughout the process of writing this book, I would be still "going to write a book" without it. Thank you to my editor Lauren Butler for her feedback, dealing with my "comma affliction" and deciphering my dyslexic ramblings. There are many other wonderful people that have helped bring this book to publication, you know who you are, and I give you my deepest gratitude. Finally and most importantly love and gratitude to my husband Lee for his never-ending love and support and who believes in me in the times I find it hard to believe in myself. To my wonderful sons Laurence and Matthew for their patience and support as I have written this book and their loving acceptance of having a quirky hypnotist and sex educator as their mum - you are my reason for doing this and I love you both.

Foreword

Womankind has been waiting for a book such as the one you are about to read. Despite making progress in parts of the world in areas of gender equality, female humans are still treading water when it comes to actualizing their own sexual freedom.

A surprisingly large portion of the female population, while enjoying success in their professional and social lives, still suffer from Puritanical restrictions over their sexual and sensual selves. This type of enslavement sustains inner conflicts that invade not only relationships with others, but with themselves.

For readers ready for self-emancipation, Kaz Riley tackles these bonds, identifies them, and then provides keys of enlightenment. With concise language that includes clear examples, she explains not only how women fell into this trap but how they can discover the pure goodness and delight of their earthly body.

The wonderful thing about change is that once a person realizes that something different is desirable, they have often experienced the opposite of change: stagnation and death. It is not ironic that *La Petite Mort* - The Tiny Death, an expression often referring to a brief, post-orgasmic loss of awareness, might also offer a metaphor from which to awaken.

Immersion in this enjoyable-to-read tome will leave you changed in wonderful ways, with a new appreciation for your capacity to embrace and accept the unlimited, wondrous nuances of sex and intimacy.

KELLEY T. WOODS
Anacortes, Washington

Contents

Embrace Techniques

Every Embrace Technique has resources such as PDFs, MP3s and MP4s available at www.kazrileywoman.com to help you.

About this book

This book intends to demystify female sexual pleasure. Give women and men a deeper understanding of everything female sexual pleasure entails and how magnificent that can be. This is not a heavy academic book, but is one that is based on over 30,000 clinical hours spanning over twenty years with my clients. I am not an academic researcher or medical doctor. I am a therapist, hypnotist and sex educator. However, I spend much of my time devouring research looking for nuggets that I can apply and utilise in a real-life, busy clinical hypnotherapy practice, with women from around the world, their partners and their sexual issues. There is now a growing body of research looking specifically at female sexuality and pleasure, but it is still far behind the research carried out on men's sexuality.

My clients have always been my most outstanding teachers; the many hours I have spent listening to, working with, and seeking to understand the challenges women experience with their sexual pleasure, is the primary source of my inspiration and the methods I have created. This book contains many of the stories my clients have shared with me and the processes I take them through as they have travelled on their journey to finding their sexual pleasure. All of my client work and the contents of this book is a combination of my experience as a therapist and the research I have found.

Sexual pleasure and sexual freedom are much more than physical things, they are about mindset and acceptance of self. Every endpoint is different. Women can embrace their sexual pleasure in many ways; it should fit with individual circumstances, beliefs, religions and lifestyles. Every person is different and so is how they experience sexual pleasure. I define sexual freedom as the ability to choose to have a fulfilling and satisfying sex life in the absence of sexual dysfunction, guilt and shame. The most important word in this definition being "choose" - we can be sexual or not, the important thing is that each woman gets to make her own choices.

This book has finally been written, after several years of me "going to write a book". The catalyst to actually do it was an overwhelming response to a video called *The big O* on my YouTube channel, *Trancing in the Sheets*. Over a thousand women from across the world have contacted me after seeing the video in the space of just a few short months. The calls and emails keep on coming a year after it was first released, now approaching 80,000 views at the time of writing this book, and increasing rapidly.

THE TERMS I USE IN THIS BOOK

For the purpose of this book, the terms Woman and Man are often referring to cis-gendered people. Especially when discussing female sexual anatomy; there will be parts of this book that are relevant to all women, but I acknowledge that there are parts that will not be. There are of course many people who identify as a woman who are not cis-gendered. Many parts of this book will still apply to these women; all women should be free of shame and guilt about their sexual pleasure, all women have eroticism and sensuality, and the source of our sexual pleasure is our minds, not the clitoris. Everyone has feminine and masculine sexual energy, both men and women have oestrogen and testosterone. This book is about helping women encompass everything about their sexual pleasure, which includes things traditionally thought of as either masculine or feminine.

This book also applies to women of all sexual orientations, straight, lesbian, bisexual, pansexual, demisexual and the many other ways women identify. This book does not infer that if you are not sexual, it makes you any less of a woman, only that women *can* be sexual if they choose. There are many ways women can express themselves sexually. As a kink-friendly therapist, my policy is that as long as good consent practices are in place and it's legal, then everyone has the right to express themselves as they see fit - don't yuck someone's yum.

I am a feminist, but I do not blame the men of today for the actions of men in the past and the history of repression of female sexual pleasure. Men have the same information we do; we cannot blame men for not having knowledge that many women do not have about themselves. As we re-educate ourselves, we must then re-educate the men. The men I work with are usually thirsty for understanding and want women to experience sexual pleasure as much as we do ourselves. For men to have that knowledge, especially knowledge about the individual women they are intimate with, we as individuals must share that knowledge and deliver that information from a place of collaborative communication. We are responsible for our sexual pleasure and we need to ask for what we need to make that happen. We also need to ask and listen to men about what they want from their sexual pleasure; from the many hours I have spent with men working with their sexual issues, it is often not what women might expect. Men also often don't know how to ask.

If you have experienced sexual trauma or abuse, there is much in this book that may help you, but it may not be enough. Many women that have endured traumatic sexual experiences benefit from 1:1 therapy of various kinds. Find a therapist you connect with and work through it. There is life after sexual trauma and its rightfully yours.

Woman is a practical book. Within it are 26 Embrace Techniques designed to help you. They cover all aspects of female sexual pleasure, some of them you will need to experience more than once, and some need to become a way of life. Like anything we do in life, practice makes perfect - keep doing them. If you have struggled with sexual pleasure for many years, it will take a little time to find, understand and embrace it. You can access further resources at www.kazrileywoman.com to help you.

CHAPTER ONE

It wasn't always this way

Sexual pleasure and sexuality is not about the physical act of having sex… it's about daring to look inward and discovering your ever- shimmering, erotic and sensual energy. It's about letting it pulse through you and your daily life, becoming part of who you are and everything you do, so that you become enchanted by the possibility of simply being yourself, a woman.

There are eight thousand glorious reasons why every woman can experience profound sexual pleasure! Most women don't know what those reasons are; for they are rarely discussed. They are not taught to us by our mothers or in sex education classes, but all eight thousand of those amazing reasons exist inside every woman on this planet.

Women and girls are still taught that our sexuality is bad; that being sexual is shameful; and that nice girls don't have sexual needs and desires! If we are taught sex ed in school, we are told about contraception, periods, unwanted pregnancy, sexually transmitted diseases and the horrors of painful childbirth. We are taught the mechanics of penetration, the *what goes where*, how to put a condom on a banana, ejaculation and the male orgasm. But there is much still missing, especially information for women and about women's sexuality. The basic information taught about women's bodies and our sexual pleasure still has many staggering gaps. We hear about our periods and are given pads and tampons, told to hide them in our bags out of sight. We are not shown how to use them, how they are inserted or what a "normal" menstrual flow is. Think about that for a second. In today's world, it is standard practice to teach teenagers how to use a condom. However, girls are still not taught how to use a tampon. In some cases, girls are discouraged from using tampons at all because "things shouldn't be put in there!"

The unique and amazing pleasure organ of our bodies - the clitoris - is omitted from anatomy textbooks like it doesn't exist. We are taught not to touch ourselves *there*, that our feelings are sinful and to lock them away. Bad things will happen to us and people will think badly of us if we are seen as less than innocent.

Even after the sexual revolution of the swinging '60s, female sexuality is still seen as something that needs to be restrained, ashamed of and controlled... but the swinging '60s was only the first stage of the reawakening (as it wasn't always this way) of women's sexual power. There is still much to be done.

Eons ago, female sexuality was worshipped. Aphrodite, the goddess of love, beauty, pleasure, passion and procreation, was a prominent force in Greek mythology. Aphrodite was syncretized with Venus, a Roman goddess. The Egyptians had Qetesh. She was a fertility goddess of sacred ecstasy and sexual pleasure. The Hindu Goddess Kunti, also known as the great "Yoni of the Universe", represented the beauty and power of the female body.

Many cultures viewed female sexuality as a glorious, powerful force, one that produced life and a source of great wisdom. Villagers gathered around campfires eagerly to listen to the wisdom of menstruating women. People travelled treacherous and long journeys to seek the help

2

of "The Kunt" (a magical and powerful healer). Every stage of a woman's sexuality was celebrated. Our cycles and rhythms were seen as magical. Female sexuality and our sexual pleasure were seen as something to be embraced, worshipped, necessary and a needed part of the very essence of being a woman. There was no shame attached to it. There is ancient art, cave paintings, and relics made from stone, shell and bone, going back as far as 35,000 BC, that shows evidence of the deepest celebration and worship, of the divine feminine, birth, menstruation and female sexuality.

But something happened over time. That great life power of female sexuality became something that was dampened, controlled and women were shamed for simply being women. In the Middle Ages, clergymen preached the idea of a woman's genitals as a potent source of evil, referring to the *Cunnis Diaboli,* meaning "Devilish Cunt".

We were told how to dress and how to behave. Any woman who enjoyed sex, sexual pleasure or masturbated was seen to be a fallen woman, slutty and unworthy.

When sex was permitted, usually only when married, it was seen as a husband's marital right, something we had to do, no matter how violent or unfulfilling it was. Women were there for their husbands' pleasure to keep them happy and for procreation. Our sexual pleasure, our orgasms and desires were seen as unimportant, with no biological use or purpose. Good sex and acceptable female sexual behaviour became not a matter for each individual woman to decide, but something that was defined by society and religion. Our sexual pleasure became shameful and wrapped in a prickly blanket of guilt, causing many women to feel deeply embarrassed about their desires and needs. Sexually, they became mute to their own needs, natural instincts and rhythms. We shut down and denied ourselves permission to experience sexual pleasure and felt guilt and remorse when we did.

The paradox, of course, is that in today's world we still hold much of that shame and fear of being branded "easy" or a slut, but at the same time are bombarded by images and opinions in the media of how we should look if we want to be desirable and that being desired is a measure of how womanly we are. That we should be sexy, but not too sexual until we *should* be sexual, and even then, we should be sexual in a particular way. How we should experience our sexual pleasure is shown to us either as romantic, un-messy and rose-tinted in blockbuster movies, or unemotional, hard and cold in mainstream pornography. It tells us how we should behave when aroused, how to "perform" our sexual pleasure and that mind-blowing, body-trembling orgasms are easy to find in just about any sexual setting. Almost all of these depictions of female sexual pleasure are telling us that our sexual pleasure is something that is given or permitted to us by others, not something we own and can create for ourselves or can enjoy by ourselves. But, if our bodies can't or don't respond sexually, if our arousal is slow to build, if we become closed down sexually in mind and body or can't orgasm, then there is something wrong with us. We are told we are cold and frigid; we are unwomanly… Simply, we are shamed when we do and shamed when we don't, and it's confusing for everyone, even our partners, who are subjected to the same conditioning about women as the women are themselves.

Every day I have the privilege of working with women from all walks of life and from every part of the world. They are married, single, divorced, cohabiting. They are professionals, academics, stay-at-home mums, entrepreneurs, artists and musicians. They are heterosexual, lesbian, bisexual and demisexual. Every kind of woman, from every kind of background, from the ages of 17 to 70. All seeking the same thing: to find their sexual pleasure and to be able to experience what they believe everyone else is. They want to know what all the fuss is about. These women are just like you.

Regardless of background, race, qualifications, age, sexual orientation, all of these amazing women have their individual stories, but tell me very similar things.

They tell me they are locked down or blocked, they feel anxious about sex and pleasing their partners. They tell me about their orgasms, or lack of them, or their inability to have them in the presence of another person. Some tell me they fear they are too old to enjoy sex anymore, others tell me of the pain they experience during sex; the pain they fear or how their vagina clamps up when they attempt penetration. They share how they fake orgasms and the embarrassment of the sounds they make when they *do* orgasm. They point to parts of their bodies they hate and want to hide. They talk to me of their frustration, their failings and why they are not desirable. They tell me of the past abusive relationships they endured and the patience of loving partners they don't want to let down. They point downward towards their vulvas, unable to even name it anything other than "down there." They talk of the worry of wanting sex too much or not wanting it at all. They are disconnected from their bodies and pleasure, they are uncomfortable in their own arousal, understand little about their bodies as receptive sexual vessels. Almost all talk of the shame they feel. They tell me they are just not good at being women.

But the truth is, all women are built for sexual pleasure. Every one of us. If you are a woman, you are built for sexual pleasure; your body, mind and natural instincts prime you for delicious, glorious sensual and sexual pleasure. When you shed yourself of the guilt and shame we often hold within ourselves, have the right information about your body and choices, let go of outdated social expectations, resolve the trauma and fear you may have experienced and give yourself permission for sexual pleasure, and embrace your sensuality and eroticism, the results are truly magical. That magic is within you, as it was always within every woman I've worked with to find and own her sexual pleasure. You just need to know how to find it. The good news is that it's easier than you might think.

Embrace and accept these statements as you read on!

- ➢ You are capable of experiencing sexual bliss!
- ➢ Your sexual energy is a vital part of your happiness and health!
- ➢ Your sexual pleasure is multi-layered - mind, body and environment.
- ➢ Sexual pleasure is not all about orgasm!

➢ Your sexual pleasure is unique and individual.
➢ You are never too old to find your sexual pleasure.
➢ Your sexual pleasure is your responsibility.
➢ Eroticism is a key part of your sexual pleasure.
➢ You are a deeply sensual being.
➢ Giving yourself permission to receive and experience pleasure is not selfish.

As you continue to read this book, I'm going to tell you things you were never taught about your body and your sexual pleasure. How your mind is the most important and profound sexual organ you have. How your body and mind can work together to give you the most wondrous sexual, erotic and sensual experiences. Some of it will surprise you, some of it will seem so obvious when pointed out, some of it you might already know. Together we will go on a journey of discovery, both inwardly and outwardly, and show you how you can find and own your sexual pleasure. I will show you how to let go of any shame you may hold, consciously or unconsciously. How to see yourself as the glorious sensual being that you are. I will show you how to connect with your sexual pleasure, to be present in your body and out of your head, so you can experience sexual pleasure alone or with a partner on your terms. It is important that you read all of the chapters in this book; each one is an important and vital piece of the sexual pleasure puzzle. At the end of our journey, you will have the tools you need to own your own sexual pleasure and have the knowledge you need to know that sexual pleasure is simply part of being a woman.

"When you make love, you try to bury yourself beneath the sheets, but the stretch marks you try to hide are proof you've survived. Your breasts are mountains not everyone knows how to climb. The goddess between your legs is the world on their tongue. She makes mouths water, your femininity is so right, like craters and waterfalls. There are few things on this side of the universe crafted with such excellence. You just so happen to be one of them."

- RUPI KAUR, *FEMININITY*

CHAPTER TWO

What is sexual pleasure?

"Anyone who is in love is making love the whole time, even when they're not. When two bodies meet, it is just the cup overflowing. They can stay together for hours, even days. They begin the dance one day and finish it the next, or—such is the pleasure they experience—they may never finish it. No eleven minutes for them."

— PAULO COELHO, *ELEVEN MINUTES*

Sexual pleasure is a glorious combination and accumulation of desire, arousal, eroticism and sensuality. It's the physical and/or psychological satisfaction, fulfilment and enjoyment derived from solitary or shared erotic experiences. These experiences include thoughts, dreams, autoeroticism, memories/past experiences and the five senses. Sexual pleasure is both a mind and body experience, and it's intoxicating stuff. When we give ourselves permission to both have and enjoy sexual pleasure, we are able to experience a vibrant array of sensual pleasure-filled adventures. Those experiences and adventures connect the body and mind and can build a joyous connection to ourselves and others.

There are a mindboggling number of words we use to describe our physical and emotional reactions to sexual arousal: libido, drive, horniness, wetness, being turned on, being in the mood, excitement, attraction, arousal, wanting, desire, lust, sensuality. Often, we use these interchangeably and without much thought about what they mean, but they're not actually the same, and the distinctions are important when you are gaining a better understanding of your sexual pleasure and what makes you tick. Confusing terms can lead to unintentional mixed messages and a breakdown in communication with ourselves and others, causing us to feel bad about ourselves, situations and our sexual pleasure.

Sexual Arousal

Sexual arousal can also be known as sexual excitement or "being turned on." It means the physiological changes that happen when the brain sends your body signals that it's time for sexual activity and pleasure. You may experience vaginal lubrication, erect nipples, and an engorged vulva or clitoris. Your heart might speed up, your upper chest and/or cheeks might flush, you might start to shiver or twitch. You might moan or make other noises. Although people talk about being "turned on," becoming sexually aroused isn't a switch in your body that gets flicked on. The way the process of arousal is portrayed in the media, especially in pornography, would have everyone believe that women go from nothing to explosive orgasms in a few minutes. But, just like any film, this is fantasy and bears little resemblance to real-life sexual arousal. Arousal is a gradual process, the seeds of which can be sown a long time before any sexual activity takes place. Every occurrence can take a different amount of time depending on if you are with someone or alone, what the circumstances are, your environment, what's going on in your life, how your day is going, medication you may be taking, how old you are and where you are in your monthly cycle if you have one.

8

Sexual arousal is often involuntary; it just happens, seemingly for no apparent reason or simply because you were thinking about something or saw something that caused a sexual arousal physical response, sometimes even by things that are not usually seen as sexual. Interestingly, it can work the other way; you can be completely, happily and willingly engaged in sexual activity or masturbation, but your body seems to be asleep; it just isn't responding, but you definitely feel aroused. It's actually completely normal. Most people will experience it, and although it can be incredibly frustrating, if you relax and let yourself feel, your body will eventually wake up, and it will usually pass.

Sexual Desire

Sexual desire is a motivational force or state. It motivates interest in sex, sexual objects, sexual pleasure and sexual activity. It can be triggered by external stimuli or internal stimuli, such as thoughts and fantasies that cause a wish or desire to engage in sexual activities. It is often referred to as "libido," "horniness," or "sex drive." Our levels of desire can fluctuate wildly and depend on all kinds of factors, from work stress to hormone levels and everything in between.

Our sexual desire can be either spontaneous or responsive. Most people I work with expect their desire to be spontaneous and that they will suddenly have a feeling or craving to have sex even with little or no sexual stimuli, which will become stronger when it's been a long time since any sexual release. Spontaneous desire is a state of being rather than a response to something or someone. Although we expect that our desire would or should be spontaneous, we are more likely to experience responsive sexual desire.

Responsive desire, when the desire to have sex is activated by some kind of physical or mental stimulation, could be from anything. A person might think they're not "in the mood" but find themselves responding to touch or thought, perhaps even a memory.

9

My favourite and the most useful way to think about desire/libido is as a "lifeforce", one that its multi-layered and caused by many things, a force that is not just about sexual pleasure, but about *all* pleasure. It is this lifeforce that gives us drive and motivates us to experience life fully with every one of our senses. Our lifeforce or libido is in a constant state of flux throughout any given day; some things feed it, and other things purge it. Our past experiences, current experiences, energy levels, hopes, fears and beliefs all influence libido. People that have lost their libido are rarely happy people. When we lose our lifeforce, we lose interest and motivation in many areas of our life. People with no libido often have high levels of anxiety, little confidence and low self-esteem. Our lifeforce and all that it encompasses is essential to our vitality, general happiness and lust for life. It is also an essential component of our ability to experience sexual pleasure. Finding and maintaining our lifeforce takes effort, we have to live our lives sensually and wholeheartedly, and we have to keep up the effort. It is no less essential to our general health than good nutrition and physical movement. You have to keep doing things to feed your lifeforce. Otherwise, it will fade away.

Eroticism

Eroticism is an essential part of our sexual pleasure. It is our personal internal world of sensual and sexual experiences and desires. Our eroticism is driven by fantasies, ideas, imagination, preferences and wishes. Our eroticism is to satisfy our needs, longings and a desire for connection. Eroticism is broader and much more complex than the desire for the physical act of sex. It is a space you enter, a place you go inside yourself, with another or others; rather than just something that you do. Eroticism is an essential part of our lifeforce. Embracing your eroticism is an essential part of finding, understanding and owning your sexual pleasure.

10

Sensuality

Sensuality is about paying attention to your senses and being present and mindful of how we sense, feel and notice our world and experiences. We have five senses: taste, touch, sight, sound and smell, and we also have "conceptual thought" in terms of our mind (i.e., what we think about). Humans are sensing beings, especially female humans. Sensuality is not always related to sex or sexuality but, to fully embrace our sexual pleasure, we must be connected to and in tune with all of our senses. Sensuality is a state of mind and a way of being. If we move through life with an awareness of our sensuality, the world becomes more vibrant, meaning we can then live a more vibrant, sensual life.

Embrace Technique

Resources available at www.KazRileyWoman.com

1. Your body as a bathtub

Erotic Bathtub

The original concept for this technique was inspired by a conversation I shared with the wonderfully talented Freja Njorden, aka "The Sensualist".

Imagine for a moment your body is a vessel than can be filled up like a bathtub. Hop into your body bathtub. Getting into the water and methodically washing your body from top to toe. You follow your usual pattern, you do it quickly to save time and with little thought. Perhaps you're even thinking about all the things you will do after your bath. You pay little attention to how your skin feels, how you are feeling inside, the temperature of the water and you don't really notice the smell of the soap you are using. You do this the same old way you've always taken a bath. Then, when you have completed your bathing routine, you pull the plug and hop out. As you dry your body you feel refreshed and clean, but your bath was nothing memorable and you probably won't be thinking about when your next bath would be.

Now imagine for a moment that your body is a glorious sensual vessel that is there to be filled with pleasure until its overflowing with delicious sensations and feelings. Imagine that everything you think and everything you do has the potential to add wonderful oils and bubbles to your erotic bathtub. You might think about your bath in advance, luxuriating in the thought of how wonderful it will be, how you might feel, how relaxing yet energising it will be, will you be alone, or will you invite someone to share your bath? Will you play music or perhaps just enjoy quiet? You draw your bath, noticing the steam rising as the bath fills and the noise the water makes as it gushes into the tub. You take your time choosing and adding in the oils and bubbles. Perhaps you light candles, turn out the lights or throw open the window to let the sun or moonlight illuminate the room. Then you climb into your bathtub, and you observe and notice how your body feels, how the water makes it feel, the sensations on your skin, the scents filling your nostrils, the light of the room reflecting off the water, the bubbles slowly popping. You surrender to the feelings and as you do those feelings steadily increase. Everything you see, hear, smell, taste and touch is like adding bath bombs of pleasure that fizz through the water, tantalising you, adding to the build-up of sensation.

You wash your body, the softness of a sponge or flannel feeling good on your skin, perhaps you notice the contrast of sensations if you switch to a brush or loofah. If you notice a particularly pleasurable sensation, you spend a little more time doing it, let your feelings and sensations guide you as to where to go next. Imagine that you give yourself permission to simply exist and luxuriate in your erotic bathtub, allowing every one of your senses to become intoxicated with the experience. You can feel the sensations surging through you, your skin tingling, you don't have to do anything except enjoy it; you're not even considering pulling the plug, it feels so good to be just right there in it. You know what happens when you will eventually pull the plug, the thought of it is delicious, the anticipation building…

Now imagine that your erotic bathtub is so full that its splashing over the sides, the sensuous pleasure is oozing out of you, it's all consuming, you simply cannot fill it anymore, you want, need and cannot wait a moment longer to pull the plug. You pull the plug, and every sensation begins to gush through it. As it does, the bathtub is still being filled with sensations, but as the sensations flow through the plug it is profoundly intense, building into an unstoppable feeling that spreads through the whole bathtub, your whole body filled with and immersed in an intense orgasmic feeling. It's a magnificent feeling, isn't it? Your body calms and the plug is closed once again. The bathtub starts filling and a residue of that experience is left behind. Slowly, it starts to fill again ready for the next time, perhaps with different oils and bubbles...

You get out of the bathtub, slowly drying your body with the softest, warmest towel. You feel so alive and happy, looking forward to the next time, perhaps wondering what combination of oils and bubbles and anything else you might add. Now ask yourself... out of those two baths,

- Which one do you want?

- Which one made you tune into your body the most?

- Which one caused the most sensations?

- Which one made you feel the calmest?

- Which one made you feel alive and invigorated?

- Which one would you want to experience again?

I would choose the second one. I'm betting you would too. So, imagine your genitals are the plug, they eventually get to have the build-up of all of that amazing pleasure rush through them, they are the destination of intense pleasure as the build of sensual erotic pleasure is released from the rest of the body. Because the body and mind are literally saturated with sensual and sexual pleasure, the feeling is spectacular. The genitals are not the source of the sensation but the accumulation of it, fed with all of the experiences of your bathtub.

Your erotic bathtub is your body. If you allow yourself to experience and feel your way through life, without judgement of those feelings and sensations, you will be constantly filling the tub, this will have a positive impact on all of your life, not just your sexual pleasure.

Access video resources related to this chapter at www.kazrileywoman.com

CHAPTER THREE

What they didn't teach you in sex education

*"It's in the reach of my arms,
The span of my hips,
The stride of my step,
The curl of my lips.
I'm a woman
Phenomenally.
Phenomenal woman,
That's me."*

- Maya Angelou, Phenomenal Woman

The view you have and how you understand your own body is essential to your physical, emotional and sexual health. The state of your relationship with your body is a vital part of how you experience your sensuality, arousal and sexual pleasure. It makes sense that if you have a very negative view of yourself mentally, physically or sexually, your sexual pleasure will be hindered by that view. The relationship you have with your sexual body starts at a very early age.

Perhaps, sometimes surprisingly, that relationship isn't related to sex or sexual pleasure. Children simply do things that feel good to them and have an innocent curiosity to discover what does.

Children touching their own genitals is normal, but it can be uncomfortable for adults to witness. How an adult reacts will impact how a child views their own body and pleasure. There are still marked social and cultural differences in how people respond to boys and girls when they touch their genitals. It is still seen as more acceptable, perhaps even expected, that boys will find their genitals and rub them simply because it feels pleasant. Boys are often told this is normal to do but something to be done privately. Attitudes are changing, but girls still tend to be told not to touch at all - that it's dirty or wrong. For many women, these early non-sexual experiences are the start of the seeds of shame and a disconnection from the pleasure their bodies can experience.

Many different sources water these seeds throughout a woman's lifetime. Social attitudes toward female sexuality still give us very mixed messages; we should be careful about what we wear, where we go, what we say, and something terrible might happen to us if we don't. The media and its portrayal of how we should look tells us that we should feel shame for our exquisite and diverse range of body shapes and sizes. Our breasts, curves and even our labia and pubic hair are questioned, critiqued and evaluated. We are taught very little about the female body and how it can experience sexual pleasure. Most of the women I work with know very little about their own body; they have many anxieties about how unresponsive it is. They have no idea how sexual pleasure works for them and even less idea about communicating this with a partner.

When we think about sexual pleasure, we often think about the sensations of the physical act of sex or masturbation. If I asked you where you feel those sensations, you might immediately think of your genitals. When I ask where those feelings originate from, many people would still say it's from their genitals. So, it stands to reason that many people focus on their genitals when they want to experience sexual pleasure. The outcome for many people doing that, is actually nothing very much at all, or it seems to take a very long time to get much effect. Many women

I work with tell me that they get frustrated at the lack of response or that it just takes too much time to get aroused. They are worrying and in a state of anxiety, their minds wandering until eventually they give up, fake an orgasm or experience an orgasm that is weak and unfulfilling. When I ask my clients about what happens during foreplay, they often talk of kissing and touching for a short while, quickly followed by oral sex leading to full penetrative sex. When they masturbate or try to, they use vibrators or fingers to create arousal.

Simply put, their focus is on their genitals. Our genitals are an essential part of our sexual pleasure, but the stimulation they require needs to start way before they are physically touched. Our genitals are the destination of multiple sources of arousal, not the source of it. It's where the focus of arousal collects and is then amplified and intensified. The origins of your arousal are varied and multi-layered and involve all of your senses. Our sexual pleasure is deeply sensual, and the female body is primed to experience it.

When we talk about the sexual body, we often think of erogenous zones as places on the body that feel good to be touched and cause a pleasure response. But erogenous actually means sensitive to sexual stimulation. That means that our erogenous zones are much more than the parts of us susceptible to touch.

Starting with the end in mind: the female genitals

Parts of female sexual anatomy are still often omitted from medical textbooks. In most books and teachings given to women, we are taught the wrong names, and our genitals are conveyed as one thing. If we use a biological term for our genitals, most often, we simply call it a vagina. From the thousands of women I have worked with, most are completely unaware of how their bodies look and function sexually. This is not their fault; it is simply because they were never taught it or were given the wrong information to begin with.

Our female genitals can be divided into three key parts:

Vagina = Opening
Vulva = External organs
Clitoris = Sexual pleasure

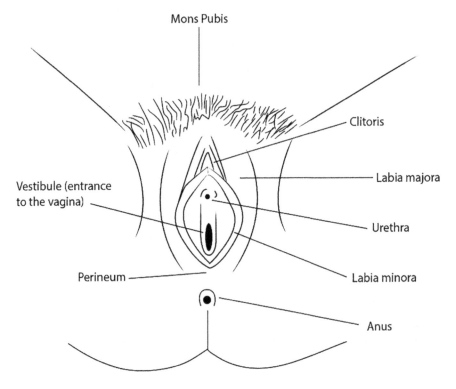

A general diagram of the female genitals

The Vulva

This is the collective name for all the external parts of the female genitals. The vulva is called lots of slang terms and pet names; often women experience crippling embarrassment talking about their vulvas and struggle to call it anything at all. In my therapy room, I have seen confident and vocal women, who can give presentations to boards of giant corporations, run companies worth multi-millions and who you would think could say or do anything, completely crumble and be utterly unable to do anything but whisper the word they use for their vulva, often whilst looking down at the floor as they do. Over the years, I have heard the vulva be called many things, and the list keeps on growing:

- Vagina (see the section below)
- Fanny (UK)
- Minge
- Foof
- Bush
- Flower
- Pussy
- Mary
- Vajayjay
- Vag
- Twat
- Wound
- Down there
- Lady garden
- Bits
- Privates
- Front bottom
- Sex
- Muff
- *Pointing silently and awkwardly towards crotch*
- Yoni
- Cunt

- The unmentionables

- Tuppence

- Line

- Kitty

- Clunge

- Minnie

- Noo Noo

- Curtains

- Coochie

- Woo-hoo

- Bajingo

This list is ever-expanding, and I continue to note the colourful, descriptive and sometimes bizarre terms my clients use for their vulva. Many of these terms are cultural or country-specific. The term *fanny*, for example, means bottom in America and vulva in the UK. Being British, I was stunned one day when an American friend offered to loan me a fanny sack, apparently to keep my personal items in when we were out walking together!

Personally, I use three terms, and as with anything, context is everything. If I am talking to my doctor, gynaecologist, or answering my children's questions, I use the term vulva. When I'm educating and working, I use the terms vulva, yoni and cunt.

Vulva – for correctness, it is, after all, what it is actually called.

Cunt – "The Cunt" was a term used for centuries to describe a woman of great power and healing. If you needed wisdom, healing, guidance, you would go and visit the Cunt. Kunti was the goddess of the female body's beauty and power; she was powerful and held in high regard. Many of the women I work with love to reclaim this term and positively use its power once they become aware of its origins. Today it is seen as one of the most offensive words in the English language; both they and I rather enjoy educating about the journey the term Cunt has taken. How can something so powerful and beautiful be offensive?

Yoni – (pronounced Yoh-nee). Anatomically, the word Yoni describes the female genital organs, including the whole outer and inner labia, clitoral and urethra area, through to the vaginal canal and includes the uterus and ovaries. Yoni has a far greater meaning than just physical anatomy. Yoni is a word that is rooted in history, societal values, mythology and our understanding of the powerful, beautiful and creative feminine energy that all women hold.

Yoni is a Sanskrit word; the very sounds of each letter have sacred meaning. In Rufus Camphausen's book, *The Yoni – Sacred Symbol of Female Creative Power*, he breaks down the sounds from the word Yoni:

Y: The animating principle, the heart, the true self within

O: Preservation, brightness

N: Lotus, motherhood, menstrual cycle, nakedness, emptiness, pearl

I: Love, desire, consciousness, to shine, to pervade, pain and sorrow

With this understanding of the term Yoni, we get a better insight into the importance and magnitude of the concepts, beliefs and profound sense of honour of the feminine creative principle. This term connects us with times and traditions which have honoured Yoni as the embodiment of divine feminine energy. Not only bringing life into the world through childbirth, but seen as having a direct connection to the Great Goddesses and the respect they commanded. The term Yoni is from a time in history when honouring goddesses was commonplace. Many of the women I work with embrace the term Yoni. It is inoffensive, powerful yet gentle, and hints at the sexual energy and potential pleasure we hold within ourselves and for ourselves. It's a term that helps women feel connected to their sexual pleasure.

What you choose to call your vulva may vary according to whom you are talking to. It doesn't matter what you call it, but do call it something. And whatever name you choose, say it with love and respect.

Vagina

Although we are taught to label female genitals as the vagina in a general sense (even the medical profession and the media use this term), the vagina is actually just the muscular canal that extends from the vulva to the neck of the cervix. The vagina is the exit for the lining of the uterus during menstruation, where a baby descends during childbirth and where penetration can occur during sex. The lining of the vaginal canal is soft and flexible. It self-lubricates during arousal and is designed to be comfortable, pleasurable and receptive.

Bartholin's glands

The Bartholin's glands are a pair of pea-sized glands found just behind and on either side of the lips surrounding the entrance to the vagina. The glands are not usually noticeable because they're rarely larger than 1 cm (0.4 inches) across. The Bartholin's glands secrete a fluid that acts as a lubricant during sex.

Skene glands

Skene glands are tiny structures that drain into the urethra. Some in the medical community believe these glands are akin to the male prostate. However, their size and shape differ significantly between women, and their exact function is unknown. Some women express liquid from their urethra when they climax. For some, this consists of a small amount of milky white fluid – this, technically, is the female ejaculate. Other women report "squirting", a much more considerable amount of liquid – enough to make it look like they've wet the bed.

The hymen myth

The hymen is a part of the vaginal opening present at birth; it is a thin layer of skin that gently covers the vaginal opening. The hymen is there to protect the vaginal opening during early infancy from infection from urine and faeces until an infant can control bowel and urine excretion. That is its only purpose! Most girls' hymens are freed from the vaginal opening during everyday active childhood life or at the onset of menstruation; it is not a symbol of virginity or purity; most women's hymens have naturally opened before puberty and a long time before becoming sexually active.

Pubic mound

The pubic mound is also known as the mons veneris, or "the mound of Venus", and is named after the Roman goddess of love.

It's a plump, rounded pad of fatty tissue that sits just above a woman's labia, the bit where most of a woman's pubic hair grows. It covers the pubic bone and acts like a bouncy cushion, which protects the bone beneath from being uncomfortably bumped and knocked during sexual activity or general life. The pubic mound is also home to lots of sebaceous and sweat glands, which produce sebum and perspiration containing pheromones, which are special chemicals designed to smell attractive to partners and provoke arousal. It includes a whole host of nerve endings which mean it can provide stimulation and arousal.

Pubic hair

Pubic hair grows on the pubic mound and around the outer labial lips, alongside the perineum and in-between the bottom's cheeks. It appears during puberty. Until the 1970s, most women just trimmed and shaped their bikini line. Nowadays, there are a vast array of options and styles, from the '70s bush to the complete removal of all hair. Have your bush how you want it (or don't) do what makes you feel good. After all, it is your pubic hair.

Urethral opening

Above and separate from the vaginal opening, simply the point of exit for urine from the body.

Labia

The labia (lips) are folds of skin around your vaginal opening. The labia majora (outer lips) are usually fleshy and covered with pubic hair. The labia minora (inner lips) are inside the outer lips. They begin at the clitoris and end under the opening to your vagina. Labia can be short or long, wrinkled or smooth. Often, one lip is longer than the other. They also vary in colour from pink to brownish-black. The colour of labia can change with age. Some people have larger outer lips than inner lips, and many have larger inner lips than outer lips. Both are sensitive and swell when you are physically aroused. There is no standard to our labia; they are as diverse and individual as we are.

Clitoris

You are built for pleasure. The tip of the clitoris (glans) is located at the top of your vulva, where your inner lips meet. It is the glans that we can see and feel externally. Every clitoris glans is a different size. It can be about as small as a pea or as big as a thumb, and the glans of the clitoris is covered by the clitoral hood. The glans of the clitoris contains over eight thousand wonderful nerve endings. To put that into context, the glans of the penis has three thousand nerve endings.

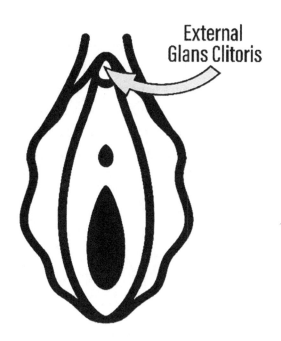

External
Glans Clitoris

The clitoris only has one function: pleasure! It is, in fact, the only part of the human body that is purely for pleasure. The male body doesn't have a "for pleasure only part." Yes, that's right... The FEMALE body is literally built for pleasure; if you are a female reading this, YOU ARE BUILT FOR PLEASURE... There are glorious things to know about your clitoris.

The glans is just the beginning of your clitoris. It is not just a little pleasure button that is hard to find; it is *much* more extensive than most people think. When I show people a life-sized model of a clitoris and ask if they know what it is, almost none do. There are some hilarious results of this question on my YouTube channel *Trancing in the Sheets*, in a video called "Nice girls don't." I even ventured out on to the streets of Amsterdam's red-light district and asked people if they knew what it was; no one did. This magnificent pleasure structure extends inside your body, back and down on both sides of the vagina. This part, called the shaft and crura (roots and legs), is about 5 inches long - yes, that's right, 5 inches!

- and about the size of the average female palm. Your clitoris is made of spongy tissue that grows bigger when you're aroused, just like the penis becomes erect. Because most of the clitoris is hidden under the skin, most women have no idea what's happening inside them as their arousal increases. The clitoris isn't hard to find, but if you don't know what you are looking for or where it is, or how big it is, it is unlikely that you will find it, let alone connect to the pleasure it can bring you.

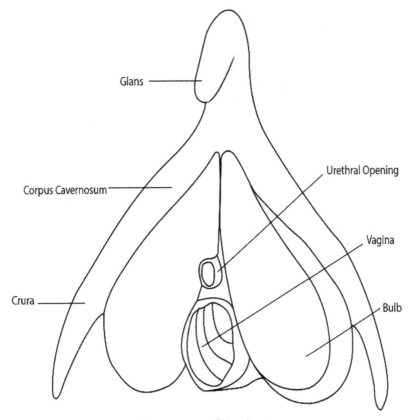

The anatomy of the clitoris

Remember, the clitoris is where our arousal and sexual pleasure becomes focused; it is not the source of it. It is the gateway to the open sea of limitless depths of sexual pleasure. Still, it needs to be supplied by constant and varied physical, emotional, erotic and sensual streams.

If your focus is just on your clitoris when attempting to experience sexual pleasure, you are forcing a response rather than inviting it. You monitor and pass judgements about its quality and level, expecting the rest of the mind and body to "switch on". This means you are always trying to get to the next stage. You are playing catch up with your own body. You are never just experiencing, but judging, and that disconnects your pleasure and anxiety kicks in.

You do need to connect to your clitoris as part of your sexual pleasure. You need to know about it, but you need to nurture it and feed it; you need to send it a stream of glorious experiences so that it responds and reacts rather than being shocked or forced into action. You are capable of reaching orgasm and high levels of sexual pleasure through thought alone or by touch that doesn't include the clitoris. Suppose you allow yourself to get to the point of desperately wanting to touch or be touched on or in your genitals. In that case, the chances are that you will be wet, aroused, responsive and ready. Your sexual pleasure will be greater and more satisfying and positively feedback into your libido or lifeforce.

Embrace Technique

Resources available at www.KazRileyWoman.com

2. Connecting with your clitoris

In the photograph below, in the palm of my hand is a life-sized model of the clitoris. As you can see, it is approximately the size of my palm. On the photograph, the model of the clitoris is facing as if it was facing outwards from your body. The tip (glans) of the clitoris is at the top (the part that sits under the clitoral hood). The roots and legs run alongside your vaginal opening.

The clitoris is about the size of your palm

If you place the palm of your hand over your vulva you can get a good idea of just how big your clitoris is. Much bigger than you probably thought.

Use this method to connect with your clitoris

- Find a place where you are comfortable and safe.

- Place the palm of your hand on top of and over your vulva. You can do this either over your clothes or directly onto your skin and pubic hair.

- Close your eyes and breathe deeply and slowly in through your nose. Release your breath slowly. Do this for several breaths.

- As you continue to breathe slowly and deeply, imagine, sense or visualise your clitoris beneath your hand.

- Imagine, visualise or sense you are sending your breath and energy down to your vulva and in particular to your clitoris.

- Imagine, visualise or sense your sensual clitoris inside you, open and receptive to your breath.

- Imagine, visualise or sense your clitoris growing in size.

- Imagine, visualise or sense your clitoris gently vibrating to the positive energy you are directing towards it.

- Allow yourself to feel a loving connection and gratitude for your magnificent clitoris.

- Privately in your mind or say out loud in a meaningful and re-spectful tone that is full of loving intent: "I am built to experience sexual pleasure."

Your sexual body

Even with its eight thousand sensuous nerve endings, your clitoris is not the only part of your body able to experience sexual pleasure. Your entire body has over seven TRILLION nerve endings and many of those nerves are involved in how you experience the world. This extraordinary internal network feeds messages both from and to your five senses. Your brain decodes and interprets those messages and tells you what you are experiencing, warmth or cold, soft or hard touch, pleasure or pain, rough or smooth, light or dark, sweet or sour and every other stimulus you encounter in your daily life. Your nervous system is a crucial part of the system that enables you to experience pleasure in unlimited and multi-layered ways.

Your body is a vessel that is able to experience the world and pleasure in a multi-sensory way, remember your erotic bathtub? Sexual, sensual and erotic stimulation is mightily more than just touch, although sensual and sexual touch is exquisite either alone or with another or others.

One of the main components of sexual pleasure is your physical sensuality. For you to experience sexual pleasure you must fully awaken all of your available senses, what you see, what you hear, what you taste, what you smell and what you touch. For some people one of their senses might always have been absent, has been lost or has changed somehow. Perhaps you have challenges with your eyesight or hearing, maybe you have no sense of smell. If that's the case for you, do not worry; your other senses will more than compensate. Also, your mind is by far your most sophisticated and vital sexual pleasure organ. What is essential is that all of your *available* senses are awake, connected to each other and connected to you, body and mind.

Your sense of touch

Touch is a sense experienced throughout your entire body, both inside and out. The variety of sensations you can distinguish through your sense of touch is unlimited. Different regions of your body experience touch in diverse and differing ways, varying in intensity and upon your personal preferences.

In today's world, touch is a sensitive subject, even more so since the onset of Covid-19, in a technology-driven and socially distanced world where so much social interaction is online. Many people are out of touch with their bodies, living inside their heads with minimal physical contact with other people. Urban living and the recent pandemic lead us to be protective of our bubble of personal space. You may have been on the receiving end of unwanted and uninvited touch. This can leave people feeling guarded and defensive towards touch in general.

Sexual, rather than sensual touch is often the only regular affectionate touch many people give and receive. Other kinds of consensual touch are now often shied away from, for fear that it may be misinterpreted or sexualised.

This fear and uncertainty around touch makes it hard to know and understand what's appropriate in every other context and what feels good to us.

But even our sexual touch is often very limited. We might explore our own or another's body, but the focus is often on lips, genitals and nipples. Your whole body can experience all kinds of pleasurable touch; you may have areas you have never explored at all.

Many of us are starved of touch, yet can have difficulty accepting touch and being comfortable with it. Touch is nourishing for the mind and body and is an integral part of life from birth. Touch relieves stress, increases bonding hormones like oxytocin, boosts your immunity and promotes well-being, trust and happiness. If you experience being touch starved, you can experience *skin hunger*, a term used to describe the unmet need for physical human contact which can be a factor in poor mental and physical health.

Your sensuous skin is the largest organ of your body and is one gigantic erogenous zone; some parts of your skin could be massively more erogenous than others, and your skin might have erogenous zones that are unique to you. How you like to tantalise your erogenous zones or have them tantalised by someone else is also very unique and personal. As you explore your skin and body, notice what feels good to you! Notice with a nonjudging curiosity how your body responds to different types

31

of touch and where. Allow yourself to experiment with temperature, texture, speed, pressure and anything else you desire. There are endless opportunities in everyday life to notice how your skin and body feels. These opportunities are not sexual, but sensual, such as:

- Touch of a partner
- The sun on your skin
- Water running over your skin in the shower
- The feel of the breeze on your face
- Sand or grass under your feet
- A warm and cosy pullover on your skin

If you give yourself permission to embrace your sensuality in everyday life with mindfulness and curiosity, not only will you be generally calmer and more confident, but you will also be waking up all of your senses and creating an exhilarating elixir to pour into your erotic bathtub when you want or need it.

Embrace Technique

Resources available at www.KazRileyWoman.com

3. Connect to your skin

A great way to connect to your skin and body is to touch all of it you can reach. Run your fingers through your hair, brush your hair slowly, run your hands slowly over your entire body, especially the parts you don't like.

Do this mindfully and with gratitude. This is your body, it tells the story of your unique journey, accept it, relish in its magnificence and love every angle, lump, bump and curve.

- Take your time.

- Focus your attention entirely on each place you explore.

- How does it make you feel?

- What feels wonderful?

- What happens if you go deeper or lighter, faster or slower?

- What happens if you add lube or massage oil?

- Calibrate your touch to your arousal, pleasure and sexual pleasure.

Erogenous zones on your body

There are endless places on the body that are very sensitive to, or can be sensitised to, affectionate, sensual or erotic touch. It can feel absolutely incredible, even on the places you rarely touch or allow to be touched. If you tend to focus all your attention on breasts, genitals, mouths, and hands during sex, or self-pleasure and masturbation, wander further and find out how you can experience touch in other places.

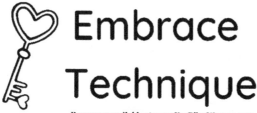

Resources available at www.KazRileyWoman.com

4. Connect with your sense of touch

On the following page is a body map with areas you can explore either alone or with a partner.

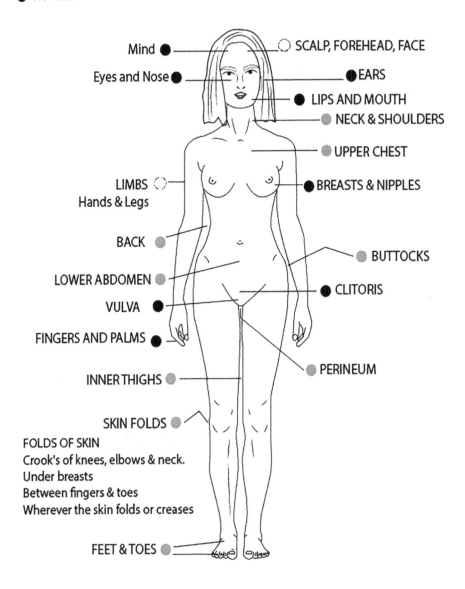

○ HOT
◔ HOTTER
● HOTTEST

Mind ●
Eyes and Nose ●
○ SCALP, FOREHEAD, FACE
● EARS
● LIPS AND MOUTH
◔ NECK & SHOULDERS
◔ UPPER CHEST
LIMBS ○
Hands & Legs
● BREASTS & NIPPLES
BACK ◔
LOWER ABDOMEN ◔
VULVA ●
FINGERS AND PALMS ●
◔ BUTTOCKS
● CLITORIS
INNER THIGHS ◔
SKIN FOLDS ◔
● PERINEUM
FOLDS OF SKIN
Crook's of knees, elbows & neck.
Under breasts
Between fingers & toes
Wherever the skin folds or creases

FEET & TOES ◔

Body Map

34

Everybody is different, and everyone has their own "pleasure map". Take your time to not only explore your body but also to experience different types of sensation.

- 🖐 **Pressure, suction and stroking**, from deep massage to light finger tracing at various speeds and intensity. Notice how the sensation feels and how you feel after differing periods of time doing this. Notice what feels good and where on your body, explore some of the lesser-known erogenous zones; ankles, wrists etc. You can do this alone or with a partner.
- 🖐 **Friction and rubbing** can feel intensely pleasurable. Experiment with different textures and materials, notice how they make you feel and how they feel on your skin - soft, silky, fluffy, hard, rough, smooth, etc.
- 🖐 **Temperature**. Notice the temperature of your skin and the contrast with things on your skin, where on your body do you like to feel coolness, heat, etc. Experiment with different water temperatures as you shower, use an oil that's warming or cooling.
- 🖐 **Erotic build-up of pleasure and sometimes pain**. Tapping, slapping and spanking can all feel fantastic and can sensitise an area. Start off gently and lightly and build up the sensation. Use your palm or the back of a flat paddle brush to do this. Notice how your skin feels to be touched there afterwards; the sensations change and the blood flow increases to the place you are tapping and endorphins are released into the body.
- 🖐 **Circling and spiralling**. Circles and spirals lightly and slowly being drawn on the skin can feel wonderful, circling around but not *on* an erogenous zone can feel incredible and will cause an intense build-up of sensation, making you crave the actual hot zone to be touched, hold out for as long as you can… good things come to those that wait. Indulge your senses, don't rush them.

Embrace Technique

Resources available at www.KazRileyWoman.com

5. *Touch connection and release of tension and emotions*

It will also identify any areas that are shut down.

- Focus on the sensations you are experiencing either during sex, masturbation, self-pleasuring, pleasurable movement or any other pleasurable experience.

- Notice each sensation without judgment.

- Let yourself feel your emotions while breathing deeply during any pleasurable activity. Emotions and tension can be held in the pelvis, hips, buttocks and vagina. When stimulating these areas with pleasure, you can release emotional tension and be open to receive more pleasure. You can release emotional tension with deep connected breathing. Focus on the part of your body that is experiencing an intense sensation or is tense. Close your eyes so that all of your attention can be focused on the part of your body that feels constricted. Breathing slowly, direct your breath into the centre of that sensation whilst putting your hand on that part of your body. Keep your mind focused on your breath as you allow emotions to bubble to the surface. Imagine them floating upward and gently popping as they are released. No judgement of these emotions as good or bad. Just allow them to be safely released.

- Give yourself permission to receive more pleasure. We often limit ourselves to what we think our bodies are capable of, or what we've been able to experience in the past. A powerful way to let go of those limiting beliefs and open the body to more pleasure is to repeat this phrase while keeping your mind focused on physical sensations: **I deserve to receive pleasure.** This gives you permission to focus inwardly and feel worthy of pleasure without it being dependent on any conditions, like pleasing your partner or reaching an orgasm. It also invites you to affirm that you are worthy and deserving of pleasure.

Your sense of smell and taste

There is a strong link between scent, sensuality and sexual pleasure[1]. Most people can detect about one trillion different odours, far more than the number of colours you can see or sounds you can hear. Studies have shown that around a third of women that lose their sense of smell experience a decrease in libido (lifeforce) and are more likely to be depressed. What you are smelling also impacts on your sexual arousal or pleasure. Scents are also attached to memories and can trigger strong feelings, emotions and even sensations in your body, from making you vomit to bliss and euphoria. Your odour sensitivity is connected with your sexual pleasure. Women with a keen sense of smell report a higher frequency of orgasms and greater sexual pleasure. So it makes sense to wake up your sense of smell and fill your nostrils with wondrous sensual aromas. There are some scents that have long been associated with sensual and sexual pleasure.

- ❋ **Lavender** is soothing and can help you relax, leading to increased feelings of arousal. Run your hand over a lavender bush in bloom and inhale the scent left on your hand. It's great in a scented candle or add a few drops of lavender essential oil to massage oil or in the bathtub.
- ❋ **Vanilla** is sweet, warm and soothing. It's also a natural aphrodisiac, connected to sexual arousal. Its sweetness can reduce drowsiness and help ease your tension and stress.

---

[1] Bendas, J., Hummel, T. and Croy, I., 2018. Olfactory Function Relates to Sexual Experience in Adults. *Archives of Sexual Behavior*, 47(5), pp.1333-1339.

- **Ginger** is spicy but sweet — the smell of ginger has been known to stimulate the circulatory system, pumping blood out to every corner of the body, especially the sex organs. Spicy and warm scents can also lead to perspiration, heightening chemicals that lead to sexual attraction. Ginger is even mentioned in the *Kama Sutra.*
- **Jasmine** has been used for erotic purposes for centuries. It contains indole — a compound that is found close to human genitals, connecting it innately to the sexual experience. It can also produce feelings of euphoria and confidence.
- **Sandalwood** has been used for over 4,000 years as an aphrodisiac. Sandalwood relieves tension, relaxes muscles and is well known for its meditative properties.
- **Amber** is warm and woody; the scent of amber creeps up as the body warms up. As an oil, amber can enhance intimacy by upping blood circulation and revitalising hormones. The scent is sultry and seductive without being too overpowering.

Taste has an enormous influence on your sexual stimulation and pleasure. Women have a higher concentration of taste buds than men, and experience taste very differently. Taste and smell initiates the mediation of your thoughts, emotions and fantasies required for arousal and sexual pleasure; taste is also a vital part of your eroticism. A smell or taste can also trigger the memory of an exciting fantasy. Women respond and react uniquely to the stimulation of taste. Your taste buds are busy 24 hours a day detecting sweet, salty, bitter and sour flavours in your food. They are also active during sexual arousal and sexual pleasure. When you exchange deep, wet kisses with a partner, your taste buds pick up on the taste of his or her lips and saliva, the latter of which can intensify arousal. You can play with taste with a partner or when alone. Notice what tastes feel sensual to you and bring you pleasure.

The eight foods commonly thought of as aphrodisiacs are:

1. Artichokes
2. Asparagus

3. Chocolate

4. Figs

5. Oysters

6. Spicy chili peppers

7. Strawberries

8. Watermelon

The scientific jury is still out on whether these foods are definitely connected to sexual pleasure, but science has come up trumps with the three foods below, with a particular focus on *women's* sexual pleasure. It seems that an apple a day can keep more than the doctor away.

* Apples. Believe it or not, apples can positively affect female sex drive. One study found that women who consumed an apple a day reported more sexual pleasure.[2]
* Red wine. A regular. moderate intake of red wine is linked to a better sexual health for women.[3]
* Saffron is often recommended as an aphrodisiac. Women taking antidepressants saw a significant improvement in sexual arousal after taking saffron in tablets or capsule form for a period of four weeks.[4]

---

[2] Cai, T., Gacci, M., Mattivi, F., Mondaini, N., Migno, S., Boddi, V., Gacci, P., Detti, B., Gontero, P., Chiodini, S., Mereu, L., Tateo, S., Mazzoli, S., Malossini, G. and Bartoletti, R., 2014. Apple consumption is related to better sexual quality of life in young women. *Archives of Gynecology and Obstetrics*, 290(1), pp.93-98.

[3] Mondaini, N., Cai, T., Gontero, P., Gavazzi, A., Lombardi, G., Boddi, V. and Bartoletti, R., 2009. Regular Moderate Intake of Red Wine Is Linked to a Better Women's Sexual Health. *The Journal of Sexual Medicine*, 6(10), pp.2772-2777.

[4] Kashani, L., Raisi, F., Saroukhani, S., Sohrabi, H., Modabbernia, A., Nasehi, A., Jamshidi, A., Ashrafi, M., Mansouri, P., Ghaeli, P. and Akhondzadeh, S., 2012. Saffron for treatment of fluoxetine-induced sexual dysfunction in women: randomized double-blind placebo-controlled study. *Human Psychopharmacology: Clinical and Experimental*, 28(1), pp.54-60.

Embrace Technique

Resources available at www.KazRileyWoman.com

6. Connecting with your senses of taste and smell

This simple method can really help you to tune into your senses of smell and taste. You can do this anywhere with any taste or smell you encounter throughout your day (obviously only taste things that are edible and smell things that are not toxic, also avoid anything you have an allergy to).

- Approach the taste or smell like you have never experienced it before. Allow yourself to pause for a moment and then either smell the scent or taste the food. Do this slowly and with curiosity.

- Notice how it tastes and smells; take your time, notice if the smell or taste changes with that time, does it cause a sensation or reaction in you?

- Allow yourself to just experience mindfully tasting and smelling.

You can do this with anything you eat or drink as you move through your day. Take some time noticing the smells as you cook with different ingredients and how they change from raw to cooked. Experiment at the fragrance section in your local department store, smell the flowers in your garden, notice the scents as you walk past eateries in your town, the smell of the sea or the park.

Your sense of sight

Your sense of sight is a powerful part of your everyday sensuality as well as your sexual pleasure and eroticism. Much of what you observe, watch, focus on or catch a fleeting glimpse of from the corner of your eye influences how you experience life and how you experience your sexual pleasure. A long-held belief has been that men are more visual than women when it comes to sexual pleasure and arousal, but the most recent studies have shown that to be untrue.[5] There is a difference between what men and women prefer to look at. Women were found to have a much greater range of visual stimuli that their minds and bodies responded to, which caused a pleasure response within them. Women reacted much more to erotic images than hard pornography; meaning they reported greater levels of arousal to videos and images of sensuality and where connection was shown between people.[6]

Maintaining a long, gentle, loving gaze into the eyes of someone you desire or care about releases oxytocin, one of the brain chemicals involved in the feelings of bonding and being connected.[7] The wonderful thing is, this also applies to looking at ourselves, especially when we give ourselves a smile. Our sight also makes the world colourful, there are many colours that are associated with sensuality, sex and sexual pleasure. Allow yourself to experience the technicolour of the world around you; it will add vibrancy to the world you have within.

- **Black** is a sexy, alluring colour associated with power and elegance. It also indicates that the person is mysterious, stylish, and authoritarian.
- **Red** is the colour of passion, romance, and lust. Known to increase blood pressure and sexually stimulating and arousing, red is considered as a sensual colour.

---

[5] Willingham, E., 2019. *Universal Desire: Men and Women Respond Identically to Erotic Images.* [online] Scientific American. Available at: <https://www.scientificamerican.com/article/universal-desire-men-and-women-respond-identically-to-erotic-images/> [Accessed 14 April 2021].

[6] Chung, W., Lim, S., Yoo, J. and Yoon, H., 2013. Gender difference in brain activation to audio-visual sexual stimulation; do women and men experience the same level of arousal in response to the same video clip?. *International Journal of Impotence Research*, 25(4), pp.138-142.

[7] Domes, G., Steiner, A., Porges, S. and Heinrichs, M., 2013. Oxytocin differentially modulates eye gaze to naturalistic social signals of happiness and anger. *Psychoneuroendocrinology*, 38(7), pp.1198-1202.

- **Pink** is also a sensual colour. It is a distant cousin of red when it comes to sexuality. However, where red ignites passion and lust, pink is all about romance.
- **Yellow** is a happy colour, optimistic and hopeful.
- **Orange** denotes feminine energy and energy of creation.

Resources available at www.KazRileyWoman.com

7. Connecting with what you see, your sense of sight

Ask yourself this, what have I seen today that held beauty? What about it was beautiful? Things you might notice are:

- A colourful flower
- A smile or look someone gave you
- A fluffy cloud in the sky
- The stars
- How the light fell on a tree or even the tree
- Someone laughing
- The steam from your morning coffee
- Children playing
- A gentle touch

This list is never-ending. We see beauty everywhere; we just don't always notice we do.

Your sense of hearing

Your sensuality and sexual pleasure can be packed with soundscapes, whispers, moans, gasps, dirty talk, squeaking beds, words of affirmation, audiobooks, music, sounds of nature and more. That sensual chorus can cause a profound response within you. But are you listening? Hearing music or sounds that you enjoy triggers the release of the brain chemical dopamine. A study of sound and touch found that listening to music you perceive as sexy or sensual actually makes pleasurable touch more arousing.[8] They discovered an overlap between the parts of the brain that process sound, and those that process touch. Hearing a partner's soundscape during sex and intimacy, when they sound authentic and spontaneous, is music to our ears, it tells us that they are getting pleasure from whatever we are doing.

We often forget that the reverse is true, the authentic sounds you make have a profound effect on your partner, but we should never "perform" our sexual pleasure, which we will look at later.

The power of simple association is also an important factor, some things sound pleasurable or sexy because you heard them in a pleasurable or sexy context and hearing them brings those memories and feelings rushing back. We all have the song that immediately takes us back to a time when we were younger and felt happy, or the song that reminds us of something emotionally painful. Our aural awareness affects how we feel and our sexual pleasure both positively and negatively.

---

[8] Fritz, T., Brummerloh, B., Urquijo, M., Wegner, K., Reimer, E., Gutekunst, S., Schneider, L., Smallwood, J. and Villringer, A., 2017. Blame it on the bossa nova: Transfer of perceived sexiness from music to touch. *Journal of Experimental Psychology: General*, 146(9), pp.1360-1365.

Resources available at www.KazRileyWoman.com

8. Connecting with your sense of hearing

- What sounds feel good to you?

- What sounds make you feel safe, calm, sensual, happy, excited?

- What do you love to listen to? Music, nature, a particular voice?

- Seek out the sounds you love, sit back and close your eyes. Use headphones if you want to.

- Just listen and notice how and where you feel it in your body.

- Bathe in the sound and become immersed in it.

- Does your breathing calm or quicken?

- Do you feel sleepy or awake?

By embracing your senses, you start to embrace yourself

By mindfully noticing the responses to all of your senses and actively seeking out new and positive ways to stimulate them in the outside world, you will create a more vibrant world within your body. Doing this purposefully will eventually become a way of life, to sense and feel your way through the world. You will become calmer, your life will feel enriched with vibrancy and when it is time to indulge in sexual pleasure, your senses will be ready and your erotic bathtub already half-filled.

To fully awaken your senses and become lost in sexual pleasure, you must also have a sense of your physical self; you need to really see yourself and embrace every single bit.

Embrace Technique

Resources available at www.KazRileyWoman.com

9. Embracing your body

- Imagine what it would be like if you had never seen a naked human body before. Suppose you had no social conditioning to think what is expected, desirable, sexy, etc. No judgement, just a curiosity of what this magnificent thing is.

- Imagine that you are discovering your body as if for the first time.

- Either imagine you are looking in a full-length mirror or actually do. Really look, notice the colour of your skin and how that changes over different parts of your body. Run your hands and fingers over your body, delight in the softness of your skin, how smooth or rough it is. Notice your hair and where that is, its colour and the sound it makes when you brush it. Notice the sensations in your hands as you do this. Cup your hands over your face and inhale how you smell, perhaps tasting too.

- Experience yourself and your body, possibly for the first time with no judgement. Dismiss any negative thoughts that may arise for now, knowing you will deal with them later. Just experience how good it feels to be seen and not judged, touched with respect, heard and not questioned. Notice what feels good, where and how you want to experience yourself using every one of your senses, allow yourself to feel and be sensual and sexual.

- Really see your physical self. Accept it and love it. Send feelings of gratitude, love and compassion towards yourself. Thank your body for the journey you have been on so far, for every breath taken, every heartbeat made, every tear you have shed and every hug it has received. Allow yourself a meaningful, internal smile at the thought of the fantastic experiences that are still ahead of you, your body is only one part of your sexual pleasure, but isn't it a magnificent one.

Access video resources related to this chapter at
www.kazrileywoman.com

CHAPTER FOUR

The Mind: your most important erogenous zone

"Mind and body are not to be taken lightly. Their connection is intimate and mysterious and better mapped by poets than pornographers."

- SHANA ALEXANDER

Your brain and mind are separate things, but they are perpetually coupled. Your brain is a physical thing that could be touched or held; your mind cannot be physically touched, as it is a set of mental faculties. Your mind is the part of you that thinks, knows, judges, remembers, reasons and learns things. It's the place where you hold your beliefs, values, preferences, thoughts, worries, morals, memories, eroticism, create fantasies and where you have an internal dialogue with yourself. What you hold in your mind greatly influences your lifeforce (libido). Your mind's activities can manifest as physical reactions and responses, and your physical responses and reactions create thoughts in your mind. Simply put, where your mind goes, your body follows - this can help or hinder your sexual pleasure and your desire to experience it.

If you experience anxiety about sexual pleasure, it's usually activated by thoughts such as "I'm not good enough", "will I orgasm?", "should I be doing this?", "I hope that I do/don't get pregnant", "is this taking too long?" or "will this hurt?". Your bodily reaction to those thoughts could be expressed as physical tension; loss or prevention of arousal; and/or not being able to let go. Sometimes you might get a bodily sensation that something isn't quite right. This sensation, in turn, activates your mind to search for the cause of that feeling. The "not quite right" feeling could have many causes, including that something isn't right! Maybe you don't want what is happening or you feel pressured; perhaps your boundaries are not being respected or are being violated. It could also be a belief that is no longer relevant to you, but still lurks in the background and becomes active in particular circumstances. Perhaps you grew up with the belief that sex outside of marriage was wrong, and consciously you don't believe that anymore, but deep down you still hold shame (of course if you believe that sex before marriage is wrong and that belief is still relevant to you, your life or religion, that is perfectly OK, we are not belief shaming here). Maybe you were shamed for self-pleasure or masturbation when you were younger; now you know it's normal and natural, but you still have shame attached to it.

The opposite is also true. When you think and feel positive about sex and your sexual pleasure and you know, understand and respect your boundaries, you will create and foster a positive feedback loop. That positive loop will enhance your experiences and make you want more. This positive feedback can also create a phenomenon called Frission, the emotional, physical response of excited anticipation when something is about to happen. You might know this feeling as "a rush."

Your magnificent mind is also your most significant erogenous zone and the one that connects all of your senses; it also has an intimate connection with your body. It can stimulate your senses into action through thought alone, like when your mouth springs into action and waters and your taste buds "remember," when all you did was think about your favourite food. Your mind can create and help you experience the most intense sexual pleasure through thought alone, even reaching orgasm without any part of your body being physically touched! Your mind is also the place that can shut you down to sexual pleasure and curb your desire. Your mind can cause psychosexual dysfunction, wrap you in a prickly blanket of guilt and shame and hold beliefs and social conditioning about how you should behave as a sexual being.

Your mind – the cornerstone of your senses

Without the influence of your mind, your senses would experience the world around you, but that information would have little meaning. You would live moment to moment from one sensual stimulus to the next, not learning and not remembering, and with no experiential memory or judgements to feed your imagination, eroticism and sexual pleasure. As we discussed in Chapter Three, your senses need to be awake and active. You need to experience the world mindfully through your senses, and when you do, amazing things start to occur and your erotic bathtub becomes continually filled.

Brain tingles and the autonomous sensory meridian response

Have you ever had the experience of watching something and feeling it (mirror touch synaesthesia)? Perhaps watching a sensual touch on a person's cheek in a movie makes your skin tingle with pleasure, just from watching? Maybe you've listened to hypnosis or guided meditation and seen pictures in your mind, created only from what you were hearing? Perhaps there are certain words you love to hear in a particular tone or from a specific voice, so much so, you tingle? Maybe you can hear colours or can taste sounds. Have you ever looked forward to something and felt that feeling of tingly anticipation as your mind creates your expectations, perhaps before a date, a massage at the spa or a long-awaited hug from someone you miss? The mind makes all of these things possible. Don't worry if you haven't experienced this. You can learn how[9]. About five years ago, a new client, Sarah, bounced into my office telling me about her love of ASMR. I had never heard of ASMR and asked her to explain. Sarah excitedly explained about the YouTube videos she had been watching and how they made her feel. She told me of the tingles she could experience and the calm it had brought her, how it had opened her to the possibility that her mind could do more than she had imagined. This had brought her to my therapy practice for hypnosis for help with her lack of libido. Fascinated by this concept, and with my curiosity on overdrive, I began to investigate how ASMR could help my clients with their sensuality and sexual pleasure. ASMR stands for Autonomous Sensory Meridian Response[10], a very geeky sounding term for a lovely tingly and highly pleasurable feeling. It usually starts on the scalp (brain tingles) and can move to any part of the body. It has taken the internet by "calm" and is an excellent resource for stress relief. One of the at-home tasks I set many of my clients looking to embrace their sexual pleasure is to explore ASMR. There are some very sexual ASMR videos available that can be a lot of fun and erotically engage the mind, but the ones I love personally and recommend to my clients are the ones that really promote sensuality and personal attention. ASMR triggers are used to cause brain tingles, calmness, good vibes and a sense of connection. The triggers are endless and fall into four main categories.

Audio ASMR triggers

- The human voice softly spoken or whispered
- Slow crinkling of paper or plastic
- Tapping sounds
- Fabric sounds

---

[9] Barratt, E., Spence, C. and Davis, N., 2017. Sensory determinants of the autonomous sensory meridian response (ASMR): understanding the triggers. *PeerJ*, 5, p.e3846.

[10] Cash, D., Heisick, L. and Papesh, M., 2018. Expectancy effects in the Autonomous Sensory Meridian Response. *PeerJ*, 6, p.e5229.

- Swishing sounds
- Pages being turned in a book
- The sounds of a keyboard tapping
- Anything the ASMR artist can think of

Observation ASMR triggers (watching)

- Hair brushing
- A massage
- Hand movements
- Unwrapping items
- Colouring and writing
- Skin tracing

Scenario/personal attention/roleplay ASMR triggers

- Hair cuts
- Makeup application
- Doctor visits
- Eye exams
- Being tucked into bed

Touch ASMR triggers (these are live and in-person triggers)

- Skin tracing
- Soft brushes on the face
- Hair play

ASMR artists usually record their videos using very sensitive microphones, and you can really become immersed in the experience by wearing headphones.

ASMR has also proven to be a vital resource for my clients who have hidden away their bodies or who have experienced trauma; helping them to reconnect with themselves, and to feel sensations and accept touch in a positive and non-sexual way. Remember, your sensuality underpins sexual pleasure. If you reclaim your sensuality, your ability to experience sexual pleasure will follow. Feeling is healing! Personally, I have greatly benefited from ASMR to help me relax and create good flowing feelings. I have noticed that the sensations have become much more intense the more I have practised ASMR.

It's helpful to use a small selection of videos repeatedly and expand the number over time. Like most things, practice makes perfect. A great resource to learn and understand more about ASMR is the book *Brain Tingles* by Dr. Craig Richard. There are numerous ASMR YouTube channels I like and my clients find useful, my favourites at the time of writing this book are *WhispersRed*, *ASMR Bakery* and *TingTingASMR*.

Embrace Technique

Resources available at www.KazRileyWoman.com

10.   *Brain tingles*

Visit my website www.kazrileywoman.com for a hypnosis and ASMR video to help you experience brain tingles and get more from our journey together. You can also find a playlist of videos from many ASMR artists that have proven to be especially helpful for my clients.

CHAPTER FIVE

Your libido is your lifeforce

When we finally give up the struggle to find fulfilment "out there", we have nowhere to go but within. It is at this moment of total surrender that a new light begins to dawn.

- SHAKTI GAWAIN, *THE SHAKTI GAWAIN ESSENTIALS*

"I have no sex drive."

"My libido is non-existent."

"I love my partner, but I've got no interest in sex."

"My partner will leave me if I can't fix my libido."

These are all statements I hear weekly from my clients. Most people view libido as a measure of how much they want sex, but it is much more than a desire measurement. Libido is the part of our personality that is considered to cause our emotional and sexual desires. Your libido is a complex thing, and it is not something that is simply turned on or off like a switch. Your libido encompasses a wide range of facets, from your emotions, playfulness and boundaries to the permissions you give yourself. It is hugely impacted by your beliefs, how worthy you feel, your hormones and even your sleep.

A much more helpful way to understand your libido and its influences is to view your libido as your *lifeforce.* A part of you that rumbles along every moment of every day, and impacts how you view the world and how you interact with it. When you start to view your libido as something much more significant than your desire for sex or sexual pleasure, you begin to understand that your lifeforce is much more about *how* you love and live, rather than a force that drives you to make love. Viewing your libido as your lifeforce also helps you to identify and then release blocks and burdens that hold you back and stop you from embracing life. The weight of limiting beliefs, shame, unworthiness and fear, can confine and define you.

These blocks and burdens create an illusion of a comfortable place; that place might be familiar, but it is also probably stagnant. Nothing ever grows in a comfort zone except frustration. Familiarity creates boredom and fosters contempt. Comfort zones hinder and stall personal growth; they prevent you from actively nourishing and tending to your lifeforce, they are also detrimental to your sexual desire and sexual pleasure.

Embrace Technique

Resources available at www.KazRileyWoman.com

11.   *Letting your lifeforce soar*

Imagine your lifeforce this way. Your lifeforce is a beautiful, gigantic hot air balloon. The balloon's envelope is vibrant with colour; perhaps it shimmers, has sparkles or has gorgeous and intricate patterns. You can change, modify and alter your balloon to your heart's desire. You can continue to alter it as you grow, as you evolve, as your tastes change or even according to how you feel on any given day. It could be an unusual shape - it truly doesn't matter, this is *your* lifeforce hot air balloon, and you get to choose exactly how it should be.

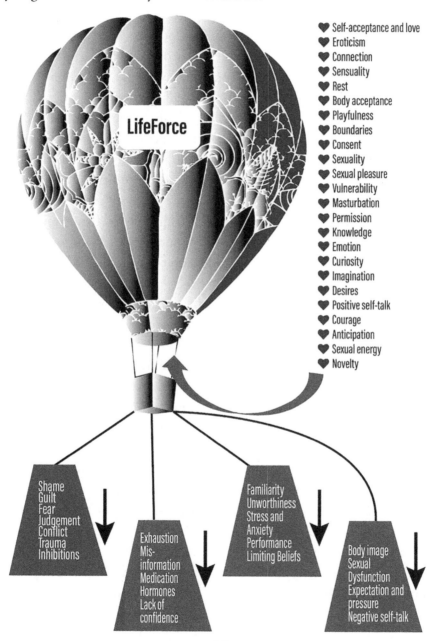

♥ Self-acceptance and love
♥ Eroticism
♥ Connection
♥ Sensuality
♥ Rest
♥ Body acceptance
♥ Playfulness
♥ Boundaries
♥ Consent
♥ Sexuality
♥ Sexual pleasure
♥ Vulnerability
♥ Masturbation
♥ Permission
♥ Knowledge
♥ Emotion
♥ Curiosity
♥ Imagination
♥ Desires
♥ Positive self-talk
♥ Courage
♥ Anticipation
♥ Sexual energy
♥ Novelty

Shame
Guilt
Fear
Judgement
Conflict
Trauma
Inhibitions

Exhaustion
Mis-information
Medication
Hormones
Lack of confidence

Familiarity
Unworthiness
Stress and Anxiety
Performance
Limiting Beliefs

Body image
Sexual Dysfunction
Expectation and pressure
Negative self-talk

Now imagine your hot air balloon needs to be inflated, so it expands outwards and upwards, loaded with your lifeforce energy, enabling your hot air balloon to fly. It is crammed with the way you experience life, your sensuality, the connection you have to yourself and others, your playfulness, desires, boundaries, body acceptance, goals, and dreams. Your balloon, filled with a wholehearted, intoxicating and glorious mix of you, is ready to take off, to be carried away by the breeze, propelled by jet streams where you can enjoy the rapidly renewing view, embrace experiences and travel to beautiful places. Your balloon is so expanded with your lifeforce energy, you can hear the ropes that tether the balloon to the ground almost creaking under the strain, as the balloon tries to take flight and soar upwards. But the balloon stays on the ground, you look over the side of the basket and you see not only tethers, but big heavy weights. Weights that keep you from taking off and flying upwards. Perhaps the weights are yelling at you, "We are keeping you grounded!" or "Flying is dangerous!" or "What will people think?" or "Who do you think you are? You can't fly!"

But something inside you tells you the weights are wrong, you can stop listening to them and you need to cut them loose, it's your time to fly...

In your basket you see a big, shiny, sharp axe. You pick it up and set to work. One by one, full of intention and with deliberate movement, you cut and sever the tethers that tie your balloon to the restricting weights. Some are easier to cut than others, some are attached with thicker tethers than the rest. Some snap and release their grip as others fall. Shame, guilt, fear, judgement, bad body image, unworthiness, negative self-talk. One after the other...cutting the ties and letting them go, as each one is released the balloon lifts a little higher. You carry on severing ties. Conflict, trauma, inhibitions, anxiety, misinformation, exhaustion...

You work hard and with focus and purpose until eventually enough of them are released, and you're taking off, rising upwards, you are flying! It's utterly exhilarating, exciting and freeing, your body brimming with your own lifeforce, keeping the balloon flying high and free. You still have your shiny axe in your basket, ready to be used with a swift and deliberate swing to repel anything trying to hold you back.

To supercharge your lifeforce, you must not only actively seek out the positive forces. You must also free yourself of everything that holds you back. If you think about this in terms of your lifeforce balloon, you could fill your balloon so much it lifts off the ground and you think you are finally on the move and getting somewhere. But to soar to new dizzying and exciting heights, you *must* let go of the things that drag you down. The same is true for your sexual pleasure.

To maintain a vibrant lifeforce, you must take care of your physical body and your mental health.

✓ Be well nourished – lifeforce requires energy.
✓ Rest - sleep is needed for vitality.
✓ Exercise - embracing life requires movement.
✓ Deal with issues - if you avoid one thing, you avoid everything.
✓ You need to know your boundaries - what is OK for you and what is not.
✓ How to say yes and how to say no, both with equal enthusiasm.
✓ Actively give consent and understand consent when it's given to you.
✓ Not worry about what other people think.
✓ Accept who you are and what that means to you.

Disruptions and fluctuations in your lifeforce

Many things can cause a disruption in her lifeforce throughout a woman's lifetime. Women are in a constant state of flux from the time they experience menarche, their first menstrual period. For most girls, this happens between the ages of 10 and 16 years of age, usually at the age of 12 years old[11]. Most women from that point go through continuous menstrual cycles (with the exceptions of pregnancy, breastfeeding, medical intervention, major life

---

[11] Lawn, R., Sallis, H., Wootton, R., Taylor, A., Demange, P., Fraser, A., Penton-Voak, I. and Munafò, M., 2020. The effects of age at menarche and first sexual intercourse on reproductive and behavioural outcomes: A Mendelian randomization study. *PLOS ONE*, 15(6), p.e0234488.

events or physical illness) until they reach perimenopause at approximately 47 and menopause at 51.[12]

If you do the maths, that's thirty-nine years of constant flux with around 500 cycles. Our menstrual cycle and where we are within it, can cause changes in our libido. In my therapists' office, women often tell me (especially when they are not taking the contraceptive pill) that their sex drive seems to change weekly or daily. There are many factors within your lifeforce that can cause these fluctuations, but your menstrual cycle plays a huge role. Most women experience a surge in their sex drive around the time of ovulation[13]. From an evolutionary standpoint, this makes sense; you are more likely to get pregnant at that time.

Women can also experience a surge in sex drive just before or during their period. The researchers are unsure why this is, and almost no research has been carried out to understand this. There is a school of thought that there is swelling in the vulva area before and during a woman's period, making the whole vulva area more sensitive and receptive to stimulation. Another school of thought about this menstrual or pre-menstrual surge in sex drive is that a woman is less likely (although it's still possible) to become pregnant at that time in her cycle, and the fear of an unwanted pregnancy is less.

A woman's sexual desire is in a constant state of flux, because our bodies are, and its completely normal. You can get a much better understanding of your cycle, by tracking it and logging how you feel, using an app on your phone, it is actually enlightening and prevents a lot of worries when you might realise that on a particular day of your cycle you rarely feel sexual and on others your sex drive is sky-high.

Many women experience a decrease in libido during pregnancy, especially during the first trimester[14]. Although we often see this referred to as sexual

[12] McKinlay, S., 1996. The normal menopause transition: an overview. *Maturitas*, 23(2), pp.137-145.

[13] Roney, J. and Simmons, Z., 2013. Hormonal predictors of sexual motivation in natural menstrual cycles. *Hormones and Behavior*, 63(4), pp.636-645.

[14] Fernández-Carrasco, F., Rodríguez-Díaz, L., González-Mey, U., Vázquez-Lara, J., Gómez-Salgado, J. and Parrón-Carreño, T., 2020. Changes in Sexual Desire in Women and Their Partners during Pregnancy. *Journal of Clinical Medicine*, 9(2), p.526.

dysfunction caused by pregnancy, it is so common that we should perhaps see this drop in libido as a normal part of pregnancy and not something to be concerned with. Once a baby arrives, adjusting to motherhood also causes enormous changes in a woman's lifeforce. Numerous factors affect sex and intimacy[15], including extreme tiredness, changing lifestyles and body image issues, leading to changes in libido. This change in libido can cause feelings of guilt and failure in women. Finding ways to stay connected, whether through sex, quality time together or working as a team, can help women and their partners navigate the transition to parenthood.

About the age of 47, our monthly cycles begin to change as we transition to a different part of our lifecycle. Perimenopause is the period of time a woman transitions to menopause (the point at which her periods stop completely). Perimenopause can begin up to eight years before menopause and bring with it many disruptions to a woman's lifeforce and how she feels about herself.

Symptoms of perimenopause and menopause are:

o periods that are heavier or lighter than normal
o worse premenstrual syndrome (PMS) before periods
o breast tenderness
o weight gain
o hair changes
o heart palpitations
o headaches
o loss of sex drive
o concentration difficulties
o forgetfulness
o muscle aches
o urinary tract infections (UTIs)
o fertility issues in women who are trying to conceive
o hot flashes
o irregular periods

---

[15] Woolhouse, H., McDonald, E. and Brown, S., 2012. Women's experiences of sex and intimacy after childbirth: making the adjustment to motherhood. *Journal of Psychosomatic Obstetrics & Gynecology*, 33(4), pp.185-190.

During the perimenopause and menopause, sex hormones in a woman's body drop. They do not, however, disappear completely. Unquestionably this drop in hormones can impact on a woman's libido and lifeforce and cause it to drop. But there is a massive difference between a lower libido and no libido. There are many elements and influences on your lifeforce and your hormones are only one of them. Many women that have not reached perimenopause who have little or no libido, the cause is not hormonal. It is the guilt, shame, orgasm focused sex, tiredness and all the other things that hold back lifeforce that are most likely the causal factors. I have lost count of the number of women I have worked with who were post-menopausal and had put their lack of libido down to their hormones. Who then left unhappy relationships, changed their lifestyle habits or let go of shame only to discover their libido came back with force, despite still being in menopause. I also regularly see women in their 60s, 70s and 80s whose lifeforce is vibrant and strong. You are never too old to experience sexual pleasure.

Find resources for this chapter at
www.kazrileywoman.com

CHAPTER SIX

Creating and calibrating your boundaries

"Daring to set boundaries is about having the courage to love ourselves, even when we risk disappointing others."

- BRENÉ BROWN

Your boundaries are an essential part of your lifeforce and your sexual pleasure. Boundaries help you identify the things you can control and influence. If you lack boundaries or your boundaries are weak, you will likely forgo your true self. You might behave and respond in a way to please, satisfy and fit in with other people's ideas and their view of the world. This can be especially true when we want to experience and express sexual pleasure. If your boundaries are weak, too porous, or non-existent, you may conform to what you *think* others expect of your sexual pleasure. This can mean performing your arousal, being on high alert with anxiety, faking orgasms, doing things you are not comfortable with, experiencing feelings of shame after the event, being coerced into something, not listening to your yes's and no's, and generally being in your head and disconnected from your body. Your boundaries help you focus purposefully and be more in control of yourself, your life, anxiety, body, and help you let go when you experience sexual pleasure. In general, I find that people struggle with setting boundaries and even more so with enforcing them.

Boundaries are not rigid and unmovable walls. They are flexible and fluid, different for varying situations and specific people in your life. If you have a robust personal boundary, you create a safe space to be freer and be your genuine and authentic self. Within your boundaries, you can affirm your inner self; your feelings, sensations, viewpoints, needs, beliefs, reactions, wants and desires.

Boundaries

| Healthy Boundaries | Limited non-existent | Loose or porous | Rigid "A wall" |

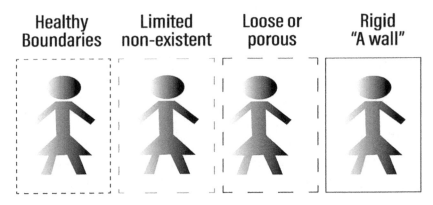

Your boundaries provide the foundation of knowledge and communication to be intimate and build strong relationships with yourself and others. By creating and calibrating your boundaries, you become aware of what is OK for you and what isn't - not only sexually, but in every aspect of your life. You become much more able to hear your own yes's and no's clearly and respect them.

All healthy boundaries have common themes. If you don't have one, you can build it.

- Your boundary needs to be solid and flexible, but is not a wall.

- You can move things in and out of a boundary.

- Your boundary may differ for different people and circumstances.

- There will be things inside your boundary that are non-negotiable.

- Only you decide what goes inside your boundary.

- You need to check in with your boundaries regularly.

- Some people might not like how your boundary affects them.

- You are responsible for your boundary.

- All boundaries require you to listen to and act upon your internal Yes and No response.

For the purpose of this book, we are going to focus on three types of boundaries: psychological, physical and sexual.

To find, understand and embrace your sexual pleasure, you need to know and embrace all three of these boundaries. Within them, you hold your authentic sexual self and within that is the freedom to embrace sexual pleasure. All three of them need you to hear and respond to your own yes and no responses.

Hearing and respecting your own Yes's and No's

You use the words yes and no all the time in daily life. We do this unconsciously and by checking in with our feelings, which may lead to differing responses depending on your preferences, likes and needs at that time and your boundaries.

For example, if a person asks if you want a cup of tea, you might respond by:

- Immediately saying no if you don't like tea or tea makes you sick.

- You might love tea but not be thirsty and say no.

- You might hate tea or tea makes you sick and say no, but then ask for water.

- You might like tea, be thirsty and say yes please.

- You might say, not right now, but I might in an hour.

Now imagine that someone just appears with a cup of tea and presents it to you. They have done this because they thought you might like a cup of tea. You might respond by:

- Feeling happy they brought you tea and accept it; you love tea and are thirsty.

- Thank them but say no thank you, you really don't like tea, tea makes you sick or don't want a cup of tea right now.

- You don't really want the tea right now, but accept it because it will make them happy, and you don't want to hurt their feelings.

- You hate tea, it makes you sick, but you accept it because you don't want to upset the other person, even though your body is repulsed by the tea and shouting at you, "Don't drink the tea!"

There might be a reason why your usual response changes, causing you to change or update your boundary. This can be difficult for other people to understand sometimes. When I turned forty, I was diagnosed with coeliac disease, and as a result, I cut out gluten from my diet entirely. It was life-changing! For the first time in my life, I felt terrific physically. All the mystery symptoms I had endured for years simply disappeared. It was easy to give up all the yummy treats I had once loved because I felt so much better, things that were once delicious to me suddenly became not so, now they made me really sick and no way was I going to eat them ever again! My body was saying no, and I was now listening. Most people accepted the change, friends and family went to great lengths to make sure that anything they offered me was gluten-free and wouldn't make me sick. I had changed my boundary according to my circumstances and what my body was telling me. One weekend, my husband and I invited some friends round for dinner. They said they'd bring dessert. "Fantastic," I said, "that would be wonderful, but if it has gluten in it, please don't be offended when I don't eat it. I was diagnosed with coeliac disease and I can't eat gluten anymore."

When our friends arrived, they brought with them the most fantastic lemon cheesecake, it looked utterly scrumptious and before my diagnosis, it was my most favourite dessert. I asked if it was gluten-free and our friends replied, "No, but it's your favourite, just once won't matter, right?"

I thanked them for bringing me my favourite dessert and told them how wonderful it looked, but sadly no, just once did matter and I would become very sick if I ate it. We ate dinner and it was time for dessert, I brought the cheesecake to the table and served up the cheesecake to everyone, grabbed some ice cream out of the freezer for myself and sat down to carry on the dinner party. I looked at my friend who was glaring at me. "I spent all afternoon making you this cheesecake, won't you even have a bite?"

I replied, "I really can't, it will make me unwell."

"But it's your favourite and I made it especially," she replied.

"No, I can't, but thank you for making it."

"Well, it didn't make you ill before," she said, rolling her eyes.

At this point I had to get firm. "We're not in the school playground, it did make me ill before, I just didn't know before that gluten was the cause."

She got agitated, telling me I had ruined her evening because I wouldn't eat the cheesecake and a real friend would have eaten it. I told her we would have to agree to disagree. Sometimes we just have to do what's right for us, even when that might upset someone else. Even if I didn't have coeliac disease, I shouldn't need to eat it if I didn't want to, just to please somebody else.

So why am I telling you this? Because as you find, understand and embrace your sexual pleasure, you may find things you now say no to, that used to be a yes, and things you say yes to that you didn't want to experience before. The important thing is that you listen to your yes's and no's. You might have been indulging in something before to please someone else, negatively impacting on your sexual pleasure, which in turn could reduce your desire and have impacted negatively on your lifeforce.

Hearing and amplifying your Yes and No responses

As I have stated several times so far in this book, where your mind goes your body follows; when you think something, you feel it in your body. It's often the body response we notice, we can and do feel our yes's and our no's. Your body responds differently to the word yes and the word no, which is known as an Ideo (idea) Motor (movement) Response (IMR). As a clinical hypnotherapist, I use this response to help my clients really understand how they feel about something or tell me how they feel without having to utter a word. I calibrate my clients to give me a yes or no response usually by a finger movement. They are often unaware of the movement; I can talk and negotiate directly with their subconscious minds to create a new path or response for them to overcome an issue. You can experience the IMR response for yourself with this simple exercise. Using a pendulum to express your internal yes and no response.

◊ Take a pendulum or a necklace with a pendant or charm on it and hold it between your index fingers.
◊ Allow the pendulum to stop swinging.
◊ Say out loud the word **YES**. Feel your yes and mean it.
◊ The pendulum will begin to move, it might swing or rotate, it doesn't matter.
◊ Now steady the pendulum again.

◊ Now say the word **No** like you mean it. The pendulum will again begin to move, the movement will be different. It might swing in the opposite direction; it might sway differently.

So why does that happen? When you express yes or no, your body responds differently, causing the pendulum to move differently. The pendulum is being moved by your body responding to your thoughts.

Resources available at www.KazRileyWoman.com

12.   *Embodied Yes and No*

The technique was the result of a collaboration with Imaginatrix

Think about a time when you said the word yes and you really meant it, this doesn't need to connect to anything sexual.

- Say the word **yes** over and over. You must really mean it and do this with conviction.
- Notice how you feel inside.
- Where do you feel the **yes** sensation in your body?
- Do you feel open or closed?
- What is your posture like?
- Is there tension in your body, if so, where?
- Are you smiling, frowning, or something else?

Now do the same with a time you said no and mean it. It's important that the memory you use is a time when your no was heard and respected. This does not need to be connected to anything sexual.

- Say the word no over and over, you must really mean it and do this with conviction.
- Notice how you feel inside.
- Where do you feel the no sensation in your body?
- Do you feel open or closed?
- What is your posture like?
- Is there tension in your body, if so, where?
- Are you smiling, frowning, or something else?

Notice that yes and no are not good and bad feelings, they are just different feelings there to tell you something, so listen to them and take note of how they feel.

Now calibrate and amplify your yes's and no's by asking yourself these questions and **feeling** the response in your body as you answer.

- Am I hungry?
- Did I sleep well last night?
- Do I like coffee?
- Do I like sunshine on my skin?
- Do I like rain on my skin?
- Do I like running?
- Is being sad fun?
- Do I enjoy swimming?

- Do I enjoy conflict?

- Do I like the taste of chocolate?

- Do I like snakes?

- Do I drink enough water?

- Do I like listening to music?

- Do I feel like crying?

Practice doing this with any question you can answer yes or no to and you already know the answer. For example, ask *do* I like (choose a food that you like or don't like), rather than ask *what* is a food that I like?

Each time feel the yes or no, after a while you will feel your yes and no without looking for it. This means when you need it in other situations, you will feel if something feels yes or no and you can act upon that feeling or in other words, you respect your yes's and no's and that helps ensure that others respect them, too.

Your psychological boundary

Your psychological boundary is just as important as your physical one, it defines your inner world from the busyness of the outer world. You can hold things within your psychological boundary that do not belong to you, stuff you have collected along the way, such as other people's beliefs and judgements, social conditioning, misinformation, and things you cannot control or influence. A great way to understand why we need a robust psychological boundary is Steven Covey's concept of the circle of concern and the circle of influence. Your circle of concern is full of the things that are inside your boundary that you have no control or influence over, they are the things that cause you to worry, have anxiety, dread and sap your energy. When my clients are focused on their circle of concern, they are usually filled with doubts and worries about things that actually have no impact on who there are as people, or how they experience sexual pleasure.

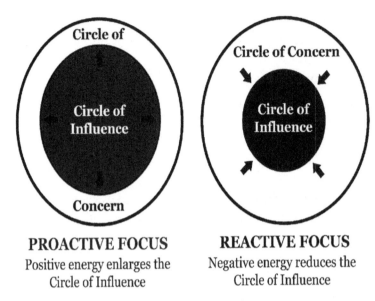

PROACTIVE FOCUS
Positive energy enlarges the
Circle of Influence

REACTIVE FOCUS
Negative energy reduces the
Circle of Influence

These concerns typically start with one of two statements:

What will people think if... (insert anything that causes a fear of negative judgement, or failure) and *What if...* (insert a negative outcome that could happen or cause judgement).

Some common statements I hear from my clients are:

- What if I can't orgasm and my partner thinks it's their fault?

- What will people think if I'm suddenly more sensual?

- What if I initiate intimacy and I get rejected?

- What will my partner think if my libido suddenly increases?

- What if a new partner finds my body disgusting?

- What will people think if they see me in the adult store?

- What if my new partner thinks I'm a slut when they find out I had an abortion when I was seventeen?

- What if my partner reacts badly if I start telling him/her about my sexual fantasies?

- What will a new partner think when they find out I'm in my forties and I've never had sex before?

- What if it comes to the crunch and I just can't do it?

When I point out to my clients that most people fear what other people might think, that actually means the most probable thing the person you are focusing on is actually thinking about this… What are *you* thinking about *them*! And even if they were thinking something unfavourable about you, so what?

What if statements need to be balanced, you can balance them with a solution-focused what if, the opposite what if. What if I can't orgasm and my partner thinks it's their fault? Well you would reassure them, wouldn't you? And what if you did orgasm and it was the most incredible thing ever? This is usually met with a nod and a "Well, yes, that's possible!" too. All of the questions, doubts and "what ifs" have only one place to be: outside of your boundary, giving you room to focus on your circle of influence.

Your circle of influence contains the things you can control and influence; how you react, how you behave, your choices, resources, knowledge, how you spend your time and many other things.

When you focus on these things you feel in control of, or could influence you become empowered, calmer and more confident. Your focus has purpose and is positive, this helps you to add things into your erotic bathtub and adds heat to your lifeforce balloon.

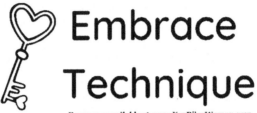

Embrace Technique

Resources available at www.KazRileyWoman.com

13.   *Creating and maintaining your psychological boundary*

- Sense, see, feel or just imagine your psychological boundary as a physical thing.

- Notice what it's made of, does it have a colour or texture? Maybe it makes a sound or vibrates. Notice that it has a way of moving things in and out. Your boundary could be anything. My boundary is a purple shimmering forcefield and I direct things in and out of it with my thoughts. If you don't have one, create one! This can be just a feeling or knowing that it's there. You don't need to see it, just imagine it's there.

- Notice how strong your boundary is and where it needs reinforcing.

- Now focus on your breathing, with every breath in, imagine, sense or feel that your boundary is becoming stronger and more defined. Keep doing this until your boundary is as strong as you want or need it to be.

- Now with every breath out, begin to move anything that is currently on the inside of your boundary that you cannot control, or that you have no influence over, such as an old habit or belief, or someone else's opinion, or anything else that serves no purpose, to the outside of your boundary. You can do this on every level, consciously and subconsciously, even just a feeling, a thought, or negative self-talk. Do this until you feel everything that needs putting outside of your boundary is now firmly outside.

- Now notice with every breath in, you can move things that are currently outside of your boundary inside, things that are helpful and you can influence. New learnings, resources, new beliefs, your own opinions, goals and dreams. Your subconscious will move things in that are helpful, but outside of your conscious awareness, that will aid you now and in the future. Continue to do this until you feel everything that needs to be inside your boundary is securely inside.

- This is both a conscious and subconscious process. It is now attached to your breathing and will continue as you move through day-to-day life, even whilst you are sleeping.

- Imagine yourself, later today, tomorrow, next week and next year with your boundary. Moving things in and out, asking yourself, should this be inside or outside of my boundary?

- Notice that with a more defined boundary you feel more confident, it feels good to enforce your boundary, you have a greater feeling of self-respect and self-worth.

Your physical boundary

You might refer to your physical boundary as your personal space. We all know that feeling when we feel someone is just a little too close, and it makes us feel uneasy. This can occur from anyone, it isn't sexual and as we discussed in Chapter Three, we can worry that just being in their personal space may be misinterpreted as sexual, or an invitation to come closer. Have you ever seen a person walk into a room that has a presence? The kind of person who draws people towards them yet has an invisible forcefield that keeps people distant? Their personal space seems almost physical around them. The people around them just sense the area and respect it. When you feel confident and connected to your body, you create a mindful and non-judging awareness of your physical self. This is a conscious state of self-acceptance, not self-consciousness. Simply, it is about being aware of your own presence in a positive way, making it much easier to project that outwardly. This happens naturally, with little or no conscious effort.

Resources available at www.KazRileyWoman.com

14. *Understanding and communicating your physical boundary for intimacy and sexual touch*

If you invite and give permission for intimate or sexual touch, or wish to touch another person, it's crucial that you know and understand your boundaries and theirs.

Physical boundaries can change over time, for example, if you become progressively more intimate with another person the areas open for physical touch may extend. You might also like to include the circumstances in which you are happy to be touched in a certain way; what you are comfortable with privately and in the supermarket are probably very different things.

Spend time considering where you are happy to be touched or touch another person. This process is helping you firm up your physical boundaries and gives the means to communicate them. There is a huge difference between welcoming touch or enduring it. This process also helps you get out of your head and into your body, stopping questions such as:

- Will they touch (body part), and I don't like it or want it?
- Is what I'm doing OK?

- Should I touch here?

- How do I ask them to touch me on my (body part)?

You can do this exercise firstly for yourself; it can be informative to realise where you are comfortable being touched, how and by whom. You can also ask a partner to do this and find out where they are happy to be touched, it helps you understand and respect their boundaries. When you know you have communicated your physical boundaries and you trust the person you are with to respect them, you can let go more easily into sexual pleasure. You know your partner has the knowledge about your body and touch that they need and you about theirs. It gives both you and them permission to explore and to know of any no go areas. This means you are more able to welcome physical touch and let go without feeling you need to be on your guard. Of course, if a person you are with then doesn't respect that boundary or tries to push more than you like, having been through this exercise with them beforehand allows you to push back more quickly. You can download and print these outlines for free at www.kazrileywoman.com. You might want to print out a few copies for this process.

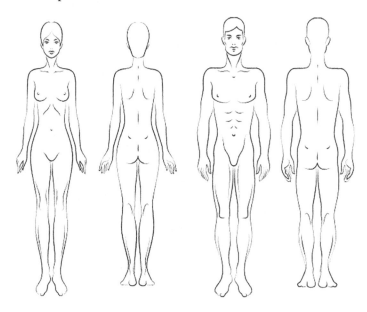

- Using the knowledge you learned from previous Embrace Techniques, think about the areas you like to be touched and mark them on the diagram. Would this be directly on your skin, over your clothes or both?

- Note any areas off-limits and mark them on the sheet (use a different colour for this).

- Consider the areas you are happy for another person to touch you (this is person-specific), again differentiate directly onto your skin, over your clothes or both, mark them on the sheet.

- Think about the areas you are happy to touch another person (again person-specific), over their clothes, directly onto their skin, again mark those on the sheet. Also highlight any areas you do not wish to touch.

- If you are doing this with a partner, now compare notes. Notice each other's boundaries, acknowledge them, state each other's no go areas and make an agreement to respect them. This gives you a much more relaxed and open container to both give and receive touch within both yours and a partner's boundary.

Your sexual boundaries and consent

An essential component of your sexual boundary set is consent. Consent is an agreement between participants to engage in sexual activity. There are many ways to give consent. Consent doesn't have to be verbal, but verbally agreeing to different sexual activities can help both you and your partner respect each other's boundaries. When you're engaging in sexual activity, consent is about communication. Giving consent for one activity does not mean giving consent for increased or recurring sexual contact. For example, agreeing to kiss someone doesn't give that person permission to remove your clothes. You can withdraw consent at any point if you feel uncomfortable. It's important to clearly communicate to your partner that you are no longer comfortable with this activity and wish to stop.

Positive consent is:

- ✓ Communicating when you change the type or degree of sexual activity with phrases like "Is this OK?"
- ✓ Explicitly agreeing to certain activities by saying "yes" if you want that to happen.
- ✓ Using physical cues to let the other person know you're comfortable taking things to the next level (words are always clearer though, or asking for what you want and if the other person is happy with that).

It does NOT look like this:

- ✗ Refusing to acknowledge "no."
- ✗ Assuming anything.
- ✗ Someone being under the legal age of consent, as defined by law.
- ✗ Someone being incapacitated because of drugs or alcohol.
- ✗ Pressuring someone or being pressured into sexual activity.
- ✗ Assuming you have permission to engage in a sexual act because you've done it in the past.

Consent is important in every relationship, even in friendships. Ask yourself, have I got fries with this?

Freely Given
Reversible
Informed
Enthusiastic
Specific

- **Freely Given.** One should never feel as if they are forced into doing anything. If consent is not Freely Given, then it is not consent.

- **Reversible.** This means that it can be taken away at any time, even in the middle of doing something you or your partner previously consented to doing.

- **Informed.** You must be informed of all activities towards which you are consenting. Consent to one thing does not imply consent to another.

- **Enthusiastic.** If someone does not seem enthusiastic about their consent, then it is not consent.

- **Specific.** Consent is specific only to a certain situation and activity. You must receive or give specific consent for each individual activity that you are involved in with another person.

Dr. Betty Martin's Wheel of Consent® takes consent and the understanding of it to a much deeper level. The Wheel of Consent distinguishes between the 'doing' aspect of an interaction; who is doing it, and the 'gift' aspect; who is it for? Asking these two questions together creates four possible dynamics, and requires a different type of consent agreement to be made. For example, if I ask a person if I can place my hand on their shoulder, and they reply, "Yes," then in traditional terms, consent has been both sought and granted. However, the Wheel of Consent says our agreement is not complete until we have also answered the question, "Who is it for?"

This is because there are many reasons why I might ask to do this:

- 🖐 I need physical contact with somebody (the touch is for me).
- 🖐 I sense that the person is in need of some physical reassurance, but I know has difficulty asking, so I initiate the offer (the touch is for them).

🖐 I'm attracted to the person, and would enjoy touching their shoulder (the touch is for me).

🖐 Perhaps I feel drawn to the clothing the person is wearing, and want to feel the texture of the fabric (the touch is for me).

THE WHEEL OF CONSENT

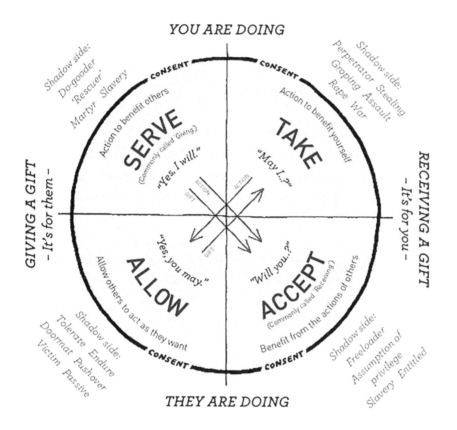

In any instance of touch, there are two factors: who is doing and who it's for. Those two factors combine in four ways (quadrants). Each quadrant presents its own challenges, lessons and joys.

The circle represents consent (your agreement). Inside the circle there is a gift given and a gift received. Outside the circle (without consent) the same action becomes stealing, abusing, etc.

Without establishing who the touch is for, it's unclear who benefits most and the reason for the request. The Wheel of Consent gives a much greater understanding and much better insight into the context of the consent. It also highlights some of the grey areas and assumptions that can accidentally occur. The Wheel works with 4 quadrants: Serving, Taking, Accepting and Allowing.

- I touch you the way you want = I am Serving
- I touch you the way I want = I am Taking
- You touch me the way I want = I am Accepting
- You touch me the way you want = I am Allowing

The four quadrants consist of two matching pairs. If I am Serving, then you are Accepting, and vice versa. If you are Taking, then I am Allowing, and vice versa. To understand the quadrants, you can consider questions people might ask when they are sharing touch, and which quadrant of the Wheel it's from.

- Serving - "Would you like me to touch you?" (it's for you)
- Taking - "May I touch you?" (it's for me)
- Accepting - "Will you touch me?" (it's for me)
- Allowing - "Would you like to touch me?" (it's for you)

The dynamics so far have the full, informed consent of both people, both are aware of who is doing, and who it is for. But the Wheel of Consent can also describe what happens in these same dynamics without consent:

- If somebody Serves without agreement, they may be people-pleasing or giving-to-get.
- If somebody Takes without agreement, they may be stealing or perpetrating.

🖐 If somebody Accepts without agreement, they may be entitled or exploiting.

🖐 If somebody Allows without agreement, they may be enduring or a victim.

With these non-consensual 'shadows' of the Wheel, you might notice which ones you sometimes find yourself in. This self-awareness can be helpful, because once you've noticed it, you can establish clear agreements based on asking, "Who is Doing?" and "Who is it for?" and "Have we both consented to that?"

Getting clarity on the difference between want to and willing to is another way of getting clear about the question "Who is it for?"

🖐 Serving = Willing to do something. "Would you like help with that?"

🖐 Taking = Wanting to do something. "Can I borrow your lawnmower?"

🖐 Accepting = Wanting to have the other person do something. "Will you brush my hair?"

🖐 Allowing = Willing to let the other person do something. "You can touch me there if you like!"

There are many different sexual activities you could potentially do with a partner. There are probably some things you really want to do, some things you're not bothered about, but would be willing to do if your partner was really into them, and other things you don't want to do, however much your partner wanted to. Similarly, your partner will have their own list. You can find out more about the Wheel of Consent and access some great video resources at bettymartin.org. Betty's book *The Art of Receiving and Giving: The Wheel of Consent* is essential reading and available on Amazon.

Yes, no, maybe lists

Starting deep and honest communication about sex can be daunting, especially in areas where we feel vulnerable. Someone might ask what you do or don't like, or what may or may not be okay with you, and you may find you have a hard time knowing how to respond. It might be particularly tough to start these conversations if talking about sex openly and out loud is something you've never done. You might find yourself feeling inclined to only say what you *think* a partner wants to hear, or only responding to what they bring up and not initiating your own questions and asking for what you want. As the final part of our boundaries and consent chapter, you might find thinking about things you want and don't want helpful, as you think about your sexual pleasure and desires. You might find things on here you've never even thought of and you can use that to fill your bathtub and feed your eroticism.

Resources available at www.KazRileyWoman.com

15.   *Yes, No, Maybe*

- Fill the list in alone and answer truthfully.

- The answers are an enthusiastic yes, a maybe or a definite no. Avoid "if it would make my partner happy" if applicable.

- If you currently have a partner or when you next enter a relationship you can ask them to fill out the list alone and then compare answers.

- No's from either party are no's, then compare joint yes answers and talk through the maybes.

There are many flavours of yes, no, maybe lists available online, covering many kinds of sex, relationship types and dynamics and just about anything you can think of.

Code Guide
Y = Yes
N = No
M = Maybe
N/A = not applicable

Body Boundaries

A partner touching me affectionately without asking first
Touching a partner affectionately without asking first
A partner touching me sexually without asking first
Touching a partner sexually without asking first
A partner touching me affectionately in public
Touching a partner affectionately in public
A partner touching me sexually in public
Touching a partner sexually in public
Having my shirt/top off with a partner
Having a partner's shirt/top off
Having my pants/bottoms off with a partner
Having a partner's pants/bottoms off
Being completely naked with a partner with the lights off or low
A partner being completely naked with the lights off or low
Being completely naked with a partner with the lights on
A partner being completely naked with the lights on
Direct eye contact
Being looked at directly, overall, when I am naked

Grooming or toileting in front of a partner
A partner grooming/using the toilet in front of me
A partner looking directly at my genitals
A partner talking about my body
Talking about a partner's body
Some or all of a disability, identity or difference I have, being specifically made part of sex, sexualised or objectified
Some or all of a disability, identity or difference a partner has being specifically made part of sex, sexualised or objectified
Some or all kinds of sex during a menstrual period
Seeing or being exposed to other kinds of body fluids (like semen, sweat or urine)
Shaving/trimming/removing my own pubic hair
Shaving/trimming/removing a partner's pubic hair
Some parts of my body are just off-limits. Those are:
I am not comfortable looking at, touching or feeling some parts of another person's body. Those are:
I am triggered by (have a post-traumatic response to) something(s) about body boundaries. Those are/that is:

Words and Terms

I prefer the following gender/sexual identity or role words (like man, woman, femme, butch, top, etc.) to be used for me:
I prefer my chest or breasts be referred to as:
I prefer my genitals to be referred to as:
I prefer my sexual orientation and/or identity to be referred to as:
Some words I am not OK with to refer to me, my identity, my body, or which I am uncomfortable using or hearing about, with or during any kind of sex are:
I am triggered by certain words or language. Those are/that is:

Relationship Models and Choices

A partner talking to close friends about our sex life
Talking to close friends about my sex life
A partner talking to acquaintances, family or co-workers about our sex life
Talking to acquaintances, family or co-workers about my sex life
An exclusive romantic relationship
An exclusive sexual relationship
Some kind of casual or occasional open/non-exclusive romantic relationship
Some kind of casual or occasional open/non-exclusive sexual relationship
Some kind of serious or ongoing open/non-exclusive romantic relationship
Some kind of serious or ongoing open/non-exclusive sexual relationship
Sex of some kind(s) with one partner at a time, only
Sex of some kind(s) with two partners at a time
Sex of some kind(s) with three partners at a time
Sex of some kind(s) with more than three partners at a time
A partner directing/deciding for me in some way with sex
Directing or deciding for a partner in some way with sex

Safer Sex and Overall Safety Items and Behaviours

Sharing my sexual history with a partner
A partner sharing their sexual history with me
Doing anything sexual which does or might pose high risks of certain or all sexually transmitted infections (STIs)
Doing anything sexual which does or might pose moderate risks of certain or all sexually transmitted infections (STIs)
Doing anything sexual which does or might pose low risks of certain or all sexually transmitted infections (STIs)
Using a condom with a partner, always
Using a condom with a partner, not always
Putting on a condom myself
Putting on a condom for someone else
Someone else putting on a condom for me

Using a dental dam, with a partner, always
Using a dental dam, with a partner, not always
Putting on a dental dam for myself
Putting a dental dam on someone else
Someone else putting a dental dam on me
Using a latex glove with a partner, always
Using a latex glove with a partner, not always
Putting on a latex glove for myself
Putting on a latex glove for someone else
Someone else putting a latex glove on me
Using lubricant with a partner
Applying lubricant to myself
Applying lubricant on a partner
Someone else putting lubricant on me
Getting tested for STIs before sex with a partner
Getting regularly tested for STIs by myself
Getting tested for STIs with a partner
A partner getting regularly tested for STIs
Sharing STI test results with a partner
Doing things which might cause me momentary or minor discomfort or pain
Doing things which might cause a partner momentary or minor discomfort or pain
Doing things which might cause me sustained or major discomfort or pain
Doing things which might cause a partner sustained or major discomfort or pain
Being unable to communicate clearly during sex
Having a partner be unable to communicate clearly
Initiating or having sex while or after I have been using alcohol or other recreational drugs
A partner initiating or having sex while or after using alcohol or other recreational drugs
I am triggered by something(s) around sexual safety, or need additional safety precautions because of triggers. Those are/that is:

Physical and/or Sexual Activities

Masturbation
Holding hands
Hugging
Kissing, cheek or face
Kissing, closed mouth
Kissing, open mouth
Being kissed or touched on the neck
Kissing or touching a partner's neck
Giving hickeys
Getting hickeys
Tickling, doing the tickling
Tickling, being tickled
Wrestling or "play-fighting"
General massage, giving
General massage, receiving
Having my chest, breasts and/or nipples touched or rubbed
Touching or rubbing a partner's breasts, chest and/or nipples
Frottage (dry humping/clothed body-to-body rubbing)
Tribadism (scissoring, rubbing naked genitals together with a partner)
A partner putting their mouth or tongue on my breasts or chest
Putting my mouth or tongue on a partner's breasts or chest
Masturbating in front of/with a partner
A partner masturbating in front of/with me
Manual sex (hands or fingers on penis or strap-on), receiving
Manual sex (hands or fingers to penis or strap-on), giving
Manual sex (hands or fingers on testes), receiving
Manual sex (hands or fingers on testes), giving
Manual sex (hands or fingers on vulva), receiving
Manual sex (hands or fingers on vulva), giving
Manual sex (hands or fingers inside vagina), receiving
Manual sex (hands or fingers inside vagina), giving

Manual sex (hands or fingers on or around anus), receiving
Manual sex (hands or fingers on or around anus), giving
Manual sex (hands or fingers inside rectum), receiving
Manual sex (hands or fingers inside rectum), giving
Ejaculating (coming) on or in a partner's body
A partner ejaculating (coming) on or in my body
Sex toys (like vibrators, dildos or masturbation sleeves
Oral sex (to vulva), receptive partner
Oral sex (to vulva), doing to someone else
Oral sex (to penis or strap-on), receptive partner
Oral sex (to penis or strap-on), doing to someone else
Oral sex (to testes), receptive partner
Oral sex (to testes), doing to someone else
Oral sex (to anus), receptive partner
Oral sex (to anus), doing to someone else
Vaginal intercourse, receptive partner
Vaginal intercourse, insertive partner
Anal intercourse, receptive partner
Anal intercourse, insertive partner
Using food items as a part of sex
Cross-dressing during sex
Having a partner cross-dress during sex
Biting a partner
Being bitten by a partner
Scratching a partner
Being scratched by a partner
Wearing something that covers my eyes
A partner wearing something that covers their eyes
Having my movement restricted
Restricting the movement of a partner
Being slapped or spanked by a partner in the context of sexual pleasure
Slapping or spanking a partner in the context of sexual pleasure

Pinching or having any kind of clamp used on my body during sex
Pinching a partner or using any kind of clamp on them during sex
Other:
I am triggered by certain sexual activities. Those are:

Non-Physical (or not necessarily physical) Sexual Activities

Communicating my sexual fantasies to/with a partner
Receiving information about a partner's sexual fantasies
Role-play
Phone sex
Cyber sex
Getting sexual images of a partner in my email or on my phone
Giving sexual images to a partner in their email or on their phone
Reading pornography or erotica, with a partner
Viewing pornography, with a partner
Giving pornography/erotica to a partner
Getting pornography/erotica from a partner
I am triggered by certain non-physical sexual activities. Those are:

By creating, calibrating, using and enforcing your boundaries, you are showing yourself compassion and respect on a physical, psychological and sexual level. By having better boundaries, you give yourself a safe place to let go of many of the blocks to your sexual pleasure. Boundaries give you space to be curious, explore, be passionate, embrace new things and to embrace your eroticism. Boundaries allow you to be receptive and open because you feel safer. You feel safer because you can set limits and communicate them, you are listening to your yeses and no's, and responding to them. This adds to your lifeforce and fills your erotic bathtub as we discussed in Chapter Two, because it allows you to focus on your sexual pleasure and everything that drives it in a positive way. In essence, healthy boundaries enhance your sexual pleasure, not prevent it.

CHAPTER SEVEN

Eroticism: your internal world of sexual pleasure

E roticism is part of your mind and is an essential aspect of your sexual pleasure and libido. It is your personal internal world of sensual and sexual experiences and desires. Your eroticism is driven by fantasies, ideas, imagination, preferences and wishes. In the words of Ester Perel in *Mating in Captivity:* "It is a space you enter, a place you go inside yourself, sometimes with another or others, rather than just something that you do."

When I ask women about how they experience eroticism, they will often answer by listing sex toys, the sexual positions experimented with, how they will wear sexy lingerie to please their partner or talk of watching porn alone or with a partner. These answers are both unsurprising and valid; all of the things they mention can be part of an erotic experience. You may have grown up with 'Position of the Week', 'How to Please Your Man in Bed', '10 Sexy Ways to Spice Up Your Love Life' and other similar articles in publications aimed at women, usually interwoven with other pieces telling you what your body shape should be and what the latest miracle diet is. Most women have been taught that eroticism is something they find outside of themselves, with the help of vibrators. Or that eroticism is about the physical act of penetration and their ability to experience orgasms. That our sexual pleasure is measured by the occurrence or absence of orgasm and how quickly that occurred. Your eroticism is much more than the collection of sex toys you might have tucked away in your bedside drawer. Don't worry; I'm not about to tell you to throw your toys away (we will cover those in a later chapter). I am, however, going to invite you to begin to view your eroticism differently and reclaim it as a place that you create inside the privacy of your mind, can go to at will and have complete control over. A place of freedom where your imagination can run unhindered, and you can experience joy, excitement and pleasure however you wish. But before you can do that, you need to know where you are reclaiming it from and what might have stopped you from embracing your eroticism in the first place.

Erotic Plasticity

"What is the greatest lesson a woman should learn
that since day one,
she's already had everything she needs within herself,
it's the world that convinced her she did not"
- Rupi Kaur, *The Sun and Her Flowers*

If you have never heard of the term erotic plasticity, you are certainly not alone, but you have it, and your erotic plasticity has been influencing your sexual pleasure!

The term erotic plasticity was created and defined by Roy Baumeister at the turn of the century [16]: "Erotic plasticity is the degree to which a person's sex drive can be shaped and altered by cultural and social factors, from formal socialisation to situational pressures. Sex drive includes

---

[16] Baumeister, R. and Stillman, T., 2006. Nature, culture, and sex: gender and erotic plasticity. *Sex and sexuality*, 3, pp.343-359.

attitudes, behaviours, and desire and is a major contributor to the overall sexual identity of the individual."

In other words, your erotic plasticity is how much your sexual behaviour and responses are influenced by your education, parental views, religion, social norms, peer group and the beliefs they lead you to hold in regard to your personal view of sex, sexuality, sexual pleasure and how you experience those things. If a person has high erotic plasticity, they are more likely to be influenced by factors from outside sources. If a person has low erotic plasticity, outside influences will have more negligible effect.

Another interesting finding of Baumeister's study is that women have much higher erotic plasticity than men, which leads to the question, why is that? There is a longstanding debate regarding the difference between male and female erotic plasticity - is it biological or cultural? As a clinical hypnotherapist specialising in sexual issues and freedom, the answer is self-evident with both male and female clients. It's cultural, and biology has very little to do with it. You might be wondering how I have come to hold this view, simply because just about every woman I work with who has sexual issues, regardless of what that sexual issue is, or how it manifests, all have one thing in common. This common theme absolutely has to be addressed for a successful therapy outcome; it is by far the biggest block to eroticism, a vital and vibrant part of sexual pleasure. That one thing is shame and the fear it brings with it.

Women's sexual shame has had endless sources and causes throughout history and has long been embedded in society. When you look at the consequences women have faced through our recent history, for simply being a woman with sexual desires, it's unsurprising that erotic plasticity is much higher in women.

Female sexuality today is still shrouded in myths, misunderstandings and the legacies of past beliefs still lurk in the background of modern society.

One of the biggest myths that is still prevalent today is that men are more sexual than women; that men have higher libidos and want sex more than women do. For a long time, studies supported this myth, mainly because if you asked women and men about desire and their sexual and masturbation habits, they gave very different answers, because society expected them to behave in different ways, so on the whole they did. How we view sex, especially women's sexuality and sexual pleasure, is influenced by the culture, politics, religion, and language of any given time in history. Attitudes towards female sexual pleasure have varied widely across different parts of the world, different communities, religious groups and cultures. Those attitudes have also changed over time. Before the sixteenth century, it was widely accepted that women were more sexual than men.

From the seventeenth century onwards, things changed dramatically, and female sexuality was repressed and controlled, mainly through fear and shame. Much of the shame associated with female sexuality and sexual pleasure from that turning point is still around today, so ingrained in society it often isn't even noticed or questioned. In the seventeenth century, religion was the most potent force, bringing with it monogamy and marriage. Marriage had connections to money, land and other material things; women's husbands were chosen for them or they were encouraged to "marry well". It had also become accepted at this time that men's sexuality was more powerful, and women were not very interested in sex. Sex outside of marriage and for anything other than producing children was deemed sinful. Adultery and homosexuality were illegal, and the punishment was death. This changed in the eighteenth and nineteenth centuries; no longer was it illegal to have sex outside of marriage, but it was still seen as sinful behaviour. Women became the gatekeepers of sex, and if we failed, we were fallen, slutty and unworthy. Sex was seen as an important part of marriage and it was also believed that a female orgasm was essential to a woman becoming pregnant. Sex became orgasm focused, but masturbation was feared to be dangerous to physical and mental health. This led to chastity devices to prevent masturbation or "self-touch" alongside the encouragement to dampen one's sexual desires and urges, especially for women, whose interest in sex or sexuality was seen by society as a bigger problem than men's.

When religion began having less of an influence on sex, psychiatry took over. In the late 1800's, sexual desire was seen as a sign of madness. Women were diagnosed with hysteria, with masturbation being seen as one of the main symptoms. The other female sexual illness was nymphomania. The symptoms of this were masturbation, sexual thoughts and fantasies, women who had sex with other women or wanted sex more than their husbands did. Women were committed to psychiatric institutions for these so-called illnesses and were seen as dangerous. They were forced to have lobotomies and hysterectomies, having their "hysteria" cut out of them; the womb was seen as the source. They had their clitorises removed, caustic chemicals inserted into their vaginas, leeches applied to their genitals and forced to sit in freezing cold baths for hours. This kind of treatment was rarely given to men and when it was only in severe cases of mental illness.

It wasn't until the 1940s that anyone studied human sexuality in a laboratory setting. That person was Albert Kinsey, who originally studied insects! Kinsey conducted hours and hours of interviews; the times were again in flux and attitudes towards sex were changing. Sex was no longer seen as a sin but as something people do and enjoy. Kinsey discovered that most people - even women - enjoyed sex and sexual tastes were varied. That sexual orientation wasn't binary, and most people are on a scale of gay to straight, with most somewhere in the middle. He also discovered that most people, men and women, masturbated.

These ground-breaking discoveries were seen as so challenging to American family values that his funding was stopped and his research projects cancelled. Remember that this was less than eighty years ago.

It wasn't until the 1960s and 1970s that the first model of sexual response or sexual pleasure was proposed. Virginia Johnson and William Masters developed the Human Sexual Response Cycle which was developed further by Helen Singer Kaplan. This research became the model to explain human sexual response and is often still used today.

Masters and Johnson also discovered that sex had both behavioural and cognitive aspects; for example, that men could lose their erections, even if they were worried they might. Literally, thought alone could cause sexual problems. These realisations were game changing. It also led to the idea that sexual problems can happen to all of us and can be overcome by understanding and different experiences.

Next came the advent of the contraceptive pill, and along with the sexual liberation of the swinging '60s also came a fresh panic about what would happen to women's sexual behaviour without the fear of getting pregnant and the shame that might bring. How were the women to be controlled? Terms like 'nymphomania', 'slut' and 'easy woman' were given new gusto and still are commonplace today.

Sexual dysfunctions were not invented until 1980 and as most of the research used to make these classifications was on heterosexual men, it's not surprising that many of these classifications of sexual dysfunction were very biased towards the male experience of sex.

In the early 2000s, a working group was formed to address the issue and reinforce that women's sexual dysfunctions were based on models created from studies on men. This working group proposed 'the new view' of women's sexuality, along with a female-centred sexual response cycle that has a greater emphasis on the social, economic and political influences on women's sexuality and sexual pleasure.[17] The group also pushed that outside sources had shaped much of how we see female sexuality and that women were different to men sexually.

The realisation finally occurred that many sexual norms for women had been pathologicalised simply because they differed from men. In the late 2000's (only twenty-one years ago) female sexual dysfunction was given its own category and female specific sexual norms were acknowledged. Of course, society takes much longer than twenty-one years to assimilate new information into the collective norm - which is why there are still

---

[17] Basson, R., 2001. Using a Different Model for Female Sexual Response to Address Women's Problematic Low Sexual Desire. *Journal of Sex & Marital Therapy,* 27(5), pp.395-403.

so many misconceptions about female sexuality and pleasure. Combine that with the ease you can access misinformation from the Internet and pornography, it's really no wonder there is still a massive knowledge gap and female sexual shame remains in the modern world today.

So, now you know that eroticism is an essential part of your sexual pleasure, and shame is a major block to accessing your eroticism. If you address your sexual shame, you will by default have better access to your eroticism and your sexual pleasure will increase.

Simply put, in the absence of shame (we will discuss how to do this in the next chapter) you can more easily access the elements of eroticism:

- ♥ Your personal freedom and sovereignty - to have bodily integrity and be the exclusive controller of your own body and life.
- ♥ The cultivation of your pleasure for its own sake and experience that how you want to.
- ♥ Capturing and maintaining your vibrancy, sensuality, vitality, life source and sexual energy.
- ♥ Reconnection with your playfulness, curiosity and mystery.
- ♥ Embracing your creativity, fantasies and imagination.
- ♥ Going outside of your usual boundaries and comfort zones and creating new ones.

Reclaiming your erotic self

"An experiment at Cambridge University showed that when numerous metronomes were placed on a stage and set off at different times, they quickly began to beat together. They are not individuals, but herd creatures connected by the rhythms and thoughts of those around them. We all have a dark side, mysterious places hidden even from ourselves. Once you allow the erotic to sweep away the conditioning, you stop ticking along with all the other metronomes."

- CHLOE THURLOW, *KATIE IN LOVE*

In a world where sexual pleasure is measured by the incidence of orgasm and based on the goal of penetration, it's no wonder that our inherent human need for the erotic has been repressed, ignored or shamed away. Eroticism is about desire, mystery, playfulness, pleasure, sensuality and your fantasies, all of which are essential streams to fill your erotic bathtub and a powerful uplifting driver of your lifeforce. In the modern world, we are taught that faster and quicker is better for just about everything, including our sexual pleasure. We focus on getting it done, reaching orgasm and everything is focused on what we believe to be the end point of our sexual pleasure. We focus on the finish instead of exploring and bathing in the hidden desires, fantasies and sumptuous processes that turn us on. Even when we are alone, we mostly know what gets 'the job' done: pornography, sex toys, focus on the genitals followed by a quick release and finish. But to truly submerge yourself in the benefits of eroticism, it can't be treated as if it is a task to be completed as quickly as possible, like we are working towards a deadline in our professional lives or a household chore. Ask yourself, what may happen if you give yourself time and space to slow down and really spend some quality time with yourself to explore? Reclaim and awaken your erotic self. Sounds like fun, doesn't it?

So far on this journey we are taking together, you have connected with your sensuality, learned new things about your body, strengthened your boundaries, and have an awareness of your shimmering and powerful lifeforce. Your mind and body connection grows ever stronger and powerful. You are giving yourself permission to become enchanted by the possibility of what you can experience and add into your erotic bathtub. Eroticism requires comfort with your own body and an attitude of playfulness and openness to exploration. It also entails a capacity for self-expression, interest in, and readiness to give pleasure and to be pleasured.

Erotica and pornography, is it the same thing?

The most-visited pornography website - Pornhub - is roughly as popular as Netflix and LinkedIn. One in five searches on the Internet are for pornography.[18] Pornography certainly has is place, but perhaps at the cost of eroticism and our imagination. As a general rule of thumb, pornography is explicit, focused on sexual acts and leaves very little to the imagination. It is about quick orgasms, watching something and is consumed by the user rather than created.

Erotica, on the other hand, can also be explicit, but is full of suggestion, mystery and creates intrigue that feeds the imagination.

The naked pole dance versus burlesque

A way to explain the difference between pornography and erotica is to compare a naked pole dance in a strip club and burlesque. Just for clarity, there is no shaming going on here, both have their place, and both can cause a great deal of pleasure for the observer and the person dancing.

The naked pole dance leaves very little to the imagination; it tends to be more direct in intention, uses exposure as a tool and is very overt in its delivery. The focus is on the nakedness of the dancer and the movements they may make.

Burlesque is about engaging the imagination, is more suggestive, invokes a sense of mystery, and uses concealment to create intrigue. The focus is on the playfulness, the eroticism and the tantalisation of the observer's mind filling in the blanks and creating the rest of the story.

When I discuss embracing eroticism with my clients, many of them immediately relate that to watching pornography. Why wouldn't they? It's very accessible. But although pornography can be both fascinating and arousing for some people, it is a very external experience; it's something you consume rather than create within. As I invite you further to view your erotic self in a new light, I encourage you to go within, use all of your senses, experiences, memories and dreams and allow your most powerful erogenous zone to assist you, your magnificent mind and all it holds.

---

[18] Covenant Eyes. 2021. *The Most Up-to-Date Pornography Statistics*. [online] Available at: <https://www.covenanteyes.com/pornstats/> [Accessed 2 June 2021].

Becoming enchanted by fantasy

Your most powerful and potent ally in your erotic world is your imagination. Within the safety and privacy of your own mind, absolutely anything goes. Your fantasies can conjure up the most powerful and erotic multi-sensory experiences, you can indulge yourself in your wildest dreams and mindscapes. Your eroticism is a key driver of your desire and can enhance your sexual pleasure to levels you may have thought not possible or ever experienced.

Many of the women I work with feel huge amounts of shame or guilt about their internal erotic world. Some common themes are:

- Am I cheating if I fantasise about a person other than my partner?

- Is there something wrong with me if I get turned on at the thought of being tied up?

- Am I unwomanly if I dream about a man being under my spell and serving me sexually as I direct him?

- Am I a slut because I fantasise about meeting a stranger and bedding him and never knowing his name?

- Am I perverted because I think about being watched as I masturbate, and it turns me on?

- I have fantasies of being raped but I would never want that in real life, am I broken?

Sexual fantasies and in fact any fantasies are a normal and natural part of adult human life. They provide escapism into another realm, one with no consequences or judgements and they are an essential part of your lifeforce. We learnt to fantasise and imagine as children, playing let's pretend games and daydreams when we were superheroes, princesses and rock stars. Our fantasies form part of our playfulness; they create intriguing and captivating landscapes within us, allowing us to explore parts of ourselves that are usually hidden or things that we may find taboo or intriguing to think about. As adults, our fantasies and daydreams are just as valid and needed in our lives, they are a vital part of having general good mental health and a key part of our lifeforce. Sexual fantasies play a crucial role in heightening eroticism and maintaining the erotic focus that is critical for sexual arousal, desire and pleasure. Fantasies are highly personal and can be incredibly diverse. Because people are unique, there is a great deal of variability in what each person finds arousing in a sexual fantasy. Fantasies are not wishes. People often fantasise about things they would never do in real life. Fantasy allows you to flirt with outrageous and totally out of character sexual behaviour without any risk of harm.

Who has sexual fantasies?

Most women have or have had sexual fantasies. They may alter with age, experience and curiosity. Dr. Justin Lehmiller surveyed 4,175 Americans about the content of their sex fantasies for his book *Tell Me What You Want* and found seven major themes that emerged. There were countless fantasies within these seven major themes. The results for the women surveyed, who reported having these fantasies at least once, are shown below as a percentage of all the women who took part in the survey.

* Multipartner sex - 87%
* Bondage, discipline, dominance, submission, sadism, and masochism (or BDSM for short) – 96%
* Novelty, adventure, and variety (doing something that's new and different for you, such as sex in a new position or setting) - 97%
* Taboo sex acts (doing something that is socially or culturally forbidden) - 72%
* Passion, romance, and intimacy (emotionally connecting with a partner or feeling loved, appreciated, or desired) - 99%
* Being in a non-monogamous relationship (swinging, polyamory, cuckolding, or having an open relationship) - 80%

❉ Gender-bending and homoeroticism (pushing the boundaries of your gender identity/role/expression and/or your sexual orientation) - 59%

Nancy Friday's books - *Women on Top, My Secret Garden* and *Forbidden Flowers* - published in the 1970s – 1990s documented thousands of women's erotic thoughts and fantasies. Covering every subject you can think of, women shared their fantasies frankly and without shame. All of these books provide both insight and inspiration to explore your own fantasies further. The internal world of fantasy, especially sexual fantasy is normal for every woman which means its normal for you too. I recommend these books to many of my clients and I encourage you to explore them too.

But I have no imagination!

This is a statement that I often hear from the women I work with. What they really mean is, I don't think my fantasies are good enough. If they are *your* fantasies it doesn't matter if they are very simple or highly elaborate, vanilla or super kinky. The only things that do matter are whether:

❉ They work for you and help you explore what works for you.
❉ You give yourself permission to have them and enjoy them.
❉ You make no judgements about them.
❉ There are many sources you can utilise to stimulate your erotic mind and get your juices flowing:
❉ Use your senses.
❉ Tap into your positive memories and past experiences of sexual experiences. These can be anything, a memorable sexual experience, past thoughts that turned you on, a flirtation you had that amounted to nothing… you can embellish them, extend them and make them yours.

❋ Notice how the things you watch make you feel - many of my clients are talking about the Netflix series *Bridgerton,* a raunchy period drama full of erotic tension, having a very positive effect. Again, anything that causes a stirring inside, anything from watching a sensual dance to pornography. Remember, the more it gets your imagination flowing, the better.

❋ Read texts or listen to audio books that you find erotic; poems, stories, erotica, anything you like!

❋ Use music that makes you feel sexy. Anything from opera to hip-hop, if it does it for you, open your ears and immerse yourself.

❋ Look at and appreciate erotic art. You can do this online, with any theme, paintings, photography, sculpture etc.

❋ Google things that interest you or you find erotic.

❋ Imagine scenarios from your answers from your Yes, No, Maybe list. Allow yourself to just imagine what that could be like; it doesn't mean you actually have to do them, try things on for size.

❋ Do things that make you feel sensual, erotic or boost your confidence. Many of my clients have taken up salsa, belly dancing and burlesque classes. Some find walking in nature or sunbathing does it for them. Wearing fabrics that feel good on their skin, or things that made them feel feminine. Several have had photoshoots done "pin up girl" style using an all-female team of photographers. I did the latter as an experiment and loved the end results and how sexy it made me feel. I have to practice what I preach, right?

❋ Do things that are just for you; go to the spa, have a long bath, take time out and have some fun, your playfulness is part of your eroticism.

❋ Use hypnosis or self-hypnosis to help you feel freer to explore your erotic self. Hypnosis can help you overcome blocks to your eroticism or facilitate an experience in your mind.

You can access many resources to help you here at
www.kazrileywoman.com

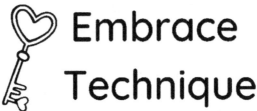

Embrace Technique

Resources available at www.KazRileyWoman.com

16.   *Your enchanting mind castle*

Enchanting Mind Castle

Imagine for a moment that within your mind is a beautiful and enchanting castle, jam-packed full of beautiful and mysterious things that can stimulate your erotic thoughts and reactions. Your enchanted castle is protected by a magical spell of absolute safety; only you can invite and choose who or what goes into your castle. Your castle is colossal with never-ending rooms, hallways, towers, turrets, basements, little quirky nooks, and snugs. Every room has different things inside, a different purpose and all are tailor-made for you. There is nothing inside your castle that would scare or hurt you. Your castle has magnificent vistas from every angle that pique your curiosity and intrigue, welcoming you ever further inside your castle. Each of the rooms are unique and are connected, by corridors, walkways, and sweeping staircases, all of them leading to extraordinary and unknown places for you to explore.

Some of the rooms are open airy and bright, others are darker with candlelight dancing playfully on the walls. Magnificent ballrooms with high ceilings, cosy snugs filled with welcoming soft sumptuous furnishings and everything in between. Sense and feel your anticipation increasing as you stand in front of your castle's entrance, waiting for the portcullis to rise and the solid door to welcomingly swing open. You can imagine giving the door a firm push. As it swings open, you feel a rush of excitement, asking yourself, what will I find here today? Crossing the threshold into your enchanted erotic world, you enter the main hall of your castle, perfectly lit with a beautiful warming light.....you notice stunning erotic paintings, photographs even intricately stitched tapestries hung on the walls. Beautiful sensual sculptures placed around the hall and an ornate fountain in the gallery creating a soothing sound as the water rises and then trickles down into the pool it sits in.

You take your time to look around the main hall, looking closely at the art and sculptures, realising as you do, that this is a gallery of your most wondrous thoughts, experiences and memories depicted on the walls. Some are of people you have never met, others a snapshot of a beautiful experience, others of things you just thought about or a *what might have been*. Some contain images of you, looking happy, sensual, comfortable in your body and free in your mind. You can feel yourself smiling, a carefree happiness inside building as you decide which part of the castle to explore first. Knowing every turn of a corridor, every staircase you climb or descend, every room you enter and every window you look out of has something exciting and tantalising to offer you, a fantasy to indulge in and adventure to be had. All of them wildly erotic, capable of filling you with exquisite pleasure, pleasure of your own creation, pleasure that is perfect for you. So explore now and treasure every single moment.

CHAPTER EIGHT

It's a shame

"An exciting and inspiring future awaits you beyond the noise in your mind, beyond the guilt, doubt, fear, shame, insecurity and heaviness of the past you carry around".

- DEBBIE FORD, *DARKSIDE OF THE LIGHT CHASERS*

Shame is one of the most influential and deeply uncomfortable emotions you experience. You feel shame when you believe you have violated or do not fit in with social norms; or that something about you makes you bad, unworthy, underserving or unlovable and you fear what others think of you as a result. Shame causes you to feel humiliated, exposed, not good enough and small, giving you an overwhelming feeling of wanting to hide or wanting the ground to open up so you can sink in and disappear. Shame turns your focus inward and causes you to view your entire self in a negative light; it's an excruciating feeling that shouts "I am bad".

Shame is different to guilt, although they are often present together. Feelings of guilt arise from a specific action or situation that you feel directly responsible for, i.e., "I did something bad." Guilt focuses your attention on the feelings of others. Women are quicker to feel shame

than men, and adolescents feel shame more intensely than adults do.
[19]Women and adolescents are more likely to experience the adverse effects
of shame, such as low self-esteem, low mood and feeling worthless.[20]

When you feel shame, you are aware that you have transgressed a
norm or at least believe you have. You must also think that the norm is
desirable, needed and binding; you won't feel shame about something you
are comfortable with and believe is perfectly fine, even if someone tries to
shame you for it. It is unnecessary for a disapproving or judging person
to be present; you need only imagine a judgment or disapproval. Often
we can conjure up an image or hear a parent, teacher, peer group, partner
or even someone we don't know asking, "You must be so ashamed?"

You might even hold a belief about a perceived social norm that you
have read about, a body ideal for example, and compare yourself so
negatively that you feel shame about your own body and want to hide it.
You can internalise criticism or judgement from others and yourself so
completely, about societal norms and expectations, that you incorporate
them into your belief systems without questioning them. Those belief
systems can impact you through your lifetime and continue to affect you
if not addressed. Sometimes the belief is an unconscious one, something
that is lurking in the background from your past. This shame can have
real staying power, even though you might have the knowledge that the
belief is faulty or untrue. When what you *know* and what you *believe*
are in conflict, it is usually the belief that wins out. Until the belief is
updated to match the new knowledge, the shame can still impact on
you. The fear of shame is a huge force that stops you doing things, this is
the fear of being judged negatively for who you are and what you desire.
When it comes to sexual shame, your shame is often misplaced.

---

[19] Orth, U., Robins, R. and Soto, C., 2010. Tracking the trajectory of shame, guilt,
and pride across the life span. *Journal of Personality and Social Psychology*, 99(6),
pp.1061-1071.

[20] Kämmerer, A., 2009. On the Intensity of Experiencing Feelings of Shame in Mental
Disorders. *PPmP - Psychotherapie · Psychosomatik · Medizinische Psychologie*,
60(07), pp.262-270.

Brené Brown defines shame in her book *I Thought It Was Just Me (but it isn't)* as "The intensely painful feeling or experience of believing we are flawed and therefore unworthy of acceptance and belonging". She also states that "Women often experience shame when they are entangled in a web of layered, conflicting and competing social-community expectations. Shame creates feelings of fear, blame and disconnection".

When we consider sexual shame, this definition gives us much insight. Women often feel they are flawed in body and or thoughts about sex. That they will not be accepted or that their desires are unacceptable. It's hardly surprising that there is so much shame present in the corners of many women's minds, when we take into account (1.) the long history of sexual shame aimed toward women; (2.) the lack of correct information we have generally in society about female bodies, sexuality, sexual arousal and sexual pleasure; and (3) the many myths in these areas that still lurk as facts.

Misplaced shame

Misplaced shame is shame that shouldn't be there. It's the shame that is based on outdated beliefs and on information that is either incomplete or incorrect. It's based on how you think things should be rather than how they actually are. Misplaced sexual shame causes anxiety (and even panic) about sexual activity and pleasure. It contaminates your erotic bathtub, takes the heat out of your lifeforce and blocks your desire, eroticism and sexual pleasure. Misplaced shame is present in most sexual dysfunctions and is often the cause of them, stopping orgasms, arousal and sometimes causing women to avoid any kind of sex, masturbation or relationship, which leads to more shame. Even sexual dysfunctions that are purely biological in cause still have shame attached to them, which can intensify them and make them worse. Rarely do I see a woman with issues finding her sexual pleasure and no shame is present. Sexual shame is so ingrained in society that when something or someone doesn't have sexual shame, they are seen as sex-positive, rather than adhering to the norm.

109

The shame women feel is evident on the answers they write on their intake forms or at consultation at my clinic. Many are not aware that they have it, almost all are hiding from it, blaming themselves and sometimes others for their lack of comfort in arousal and pleasure.

Here are some of the statements I see and hear regularly from my clients:

- I am not able to orgasm with my partner. I can orgasm alone. This is affecting his self-esteem and he says he's never had this problem before.
- When my partner goes down on me, I'm thinking, *this is taking too long, is he bored, does he even enjoy this?*
- I have no libido; I just don't want sex. My husband is a loving and caring man but I'm afraid he will leave me or have an affair.
- I was raped when I was eighteen by a so-called friend, I just got on with it and felt OK. I told a friend recently about this and she thinks I need therapy because no one is okay after that.
- I had an abortion in my twenties, am I being punished now so I don't enjoy sex?
- Look at me, who would want this?
- I'm forty-six and a virgin, how can I possibly tell anyone that? They would think I'm a freak, so as soon as a relationship gets to the point where sex is on the cards, I run away.
- Sex hurts, everything clamps up. My partner says he doesn't want to hurt me, so we've stopped even trying, what kind of a woman does that make me?
- My parents could not accept I was gay, so I went with boys, I pretended to like it, but it was awful.
- When I was eighteen, I fell in love and got pregnant. I was sent to a mother and baby home for my pregnancy until I gave birth. The home was run by nuns who told me I was wicked; I gave birth to my son and they took him away. I was sent home to my parents,

they had told everyone I was away working, they never spoke of my baby or spoke much to me when I returned.

- My partner had an affair, I'm sure if I had been better at sex, it wouldn't have happened.

- I was caught masturbating when I was thirteen by my mother, she screamed, "Don't touch yourself there!" and that I was dirty.

- I was told that if I ever got pregnant, I would be disowned and it would bring great shame to my family. I've now been married for three years and I'm still very tense about sex; I feel like I am doing something wrong.

- I was seventeen the first time I had sex and I caught herpes, I haven't had sex since. I'm too ashamed to tell anyone I have it, who would believe I had only had sex once?

- I had sex with a boy when I was fifteen; he told the whole school, the other kids taunted me, calling me a slut.

- I was sexually abused by my father, my mother said I must have done something to cause that because he is a good man.

- My labia are all wrong, my flaps hang out. I'm too embarrassed to show anyone.

- I'm not normal, it takes ages for me to get aroused, I feel really self-conscious and can't let go.

- I have fantasies about dominating a man and making him do things to me sexually, is this normal?

- I slept around when I was at university, I loved sex, but now I feel nothing at all.

- I had a mastectomy and I don't feel like a woman anymore. My partner tells me I'm beautiful, but I don't believe him.

- My husband thinks I don't want him or enjoy sex because I never ask for it, I just don't know how to ask.

- I get too wet, it's embarrassing.

- I have a much higher sex drive than my boyfriend, he says I'm not normal and something must have happened to me, for me to be this way.

111

☐ I've faked my orgasms for years with my partner. I can cum on my own, but I never have with him, it's like an act and I don't enjoy it anymore and I hate lying to him.

Overcoming misplaced sexual shame and reclaiming your sexual pleasure

Recognise the shame

Evaluate the source and origins

Courage to challenge and change

Let the past belief go

Accept the new understanding

Internalise

Move forward

R.E.C.L.A.I.M

Recognise the shame

So now you know that you are reclaiming your sexual pleasure from shame and that shame is usually misplaced. You also need to be aware when you are feeling shame. Sometimes, you can become so enveloped in self-blame and unworthiness. The fact you are feeling those things because of misplaced shame passes you by, you simply don't recognise it as shame. This means the feelings of shame you have makes no sense to you. You can even think you have no issues around sex or sexual pleasure and that you no longer believe things that you might have believed in the past –

sex is bad, women can't be sexual, etc. When this happens, it can be hard to know why you feel the way you do, or what might be at the root of it, which makes it even harder to overcome. When you are reclaiming your sexual pleasure from shame, the first thing we have to do is to recognise it.

6 areas to help you identify that you may have sexual shame

Insecurity with the self

- Disconnection from the body, sensuality or eroticism.
- Feelings of anxiety during sex or when thinking about it.
- Poor body image.
- Negative self-talk about your body or genitals.
- Wanting to hide away.
- Not listening to your yes's and no's.

Uncomfortable physical feelings or diminished voice

- Struggle to make or hold eye contact with partners.
- Crossing your arms over your body in a protective way.
- Feeling uncomfortable expressing sexual desires and needs.
- Concerns about making sexual noises.
- Negative self-talk about desires.

Sexual dysfunction and dissatisfaction

- Painful sex.
- Anorgasmia (not being able to orgasm).
- Disconnection.
- Lack of arousal.
- Feeling frustrated.
- Lack of desire.
- Lack of natural lubrication.
- Wanting to get sex over and done with.

Trouble with intimacy and relationships

- ☐ Avoidance.
- ☐ Being shut down.
- ☐ Feeling inhibited.
- ☐ Not feeling good enough.

Viewing sex or masturbation as "bad" or something that you "shouldn't do"

- ☐ Experiencing feelings of regret and shame immediately after any sexual activity.
- ☐ Feeling bad about sexual fantasies.
- ☐ Feeling bad about experiencing sexual pleasure.
- ☐ Feeling uncomfortable mentally when aroused.
- ☐ Feeling dirty or like you are doing something wrong.
- ☐ Feeling uncomfortable touching your own genitals.

Uncomfortable talking about sex

- ☐ Feeling nervous, or a deep burning embarrassment, when the topic of sex comes up.
- ☐ Not being able to express needs and desires.
- ☐ Feeling dirty when discussing sex.
- ☐ Feeling uncomfortable when asked about sex by a doctor, etc.

Once you have recognised that you may be experiencing misplaced shame, it becomes much easier to deal with, because then you can start to question, should I have this, what can I do about this? It makes you start to look for the knowledge and solution, rather than feeling like you are drowning in a sea of shame.

Evaluate the source and origins

Once you have identified that you are experiencing shame, and that the sexual shame is most likely misplaced (you can assume that it is misplaced, because it always is). You need to evaluate the shame's sources and origins.

Ask yourself: is this your belief or opinion, or someone else's?

When I ask this question to my clients, they often look confused and ask me what I mean. When Sarah visited my office she was concerned that there was something wrong with her. She was worried that she liked sex too much. During her consultation she told me that when she was seven years old she had been sexually abused by a family member and put into foster care as a result. She lived with her foster family until she gained a place at university where she was now studying to become a social worker. She had a steady boyfriend and had had a great sex life until three months ago. During a lecture at university, the subject of sexual abuse in families was being discussed, and Sarah disclosed her own background. After the lecture in the student coffee shop, one of her peers had questioned her, "If she had been sexually abused as a child, how could she possibly be in a relationship and how could she even consider having sex?"

Sarah replied that, the abuse was a long time ago and that she actually really enjoyed sex. Her peer replied, "Well, you shouldn't. How could you, after what happened to you? You are in denial, you need to get help".

Since that conversation, every time Sarah was having sex with her boyfriend, she found herself feeling ashamed that she liked it, full of doubt and regret afterwards, and started wondering that perhaps something *was* wrong with her. Sarah looked very frightened as she asked, "Am I broken, I shouldn't want sex after what happened to me, should I?"

I asked her this: "I see women here every week that have been sexually abused, assaulted or harassed, in fact I would be hard pushed to find a woman who hasn't at least been made to feel very uncomfortable at least once in her lifetime. If we are to believe your friend, are we to say that none of us should enjoy sex or be in relationships because of someone else's actions?"

"Of course not," she replied. We discussed how some people would have issues in later life after being abused and we do our best to help them overcome that; we do that because we believe that they can overcome the trauma and go on to have fulfilling sex lives. The fact that she could have a wonderful time sexually was something to be celebrated, not something to be shamed for.

During her session we did some work connecting her with her younger and future self, celebrated her connection with her body and her good sexual experiences. I watched as relief washed over her as she let the shame go. As she left, I told her to give her peer my business card because the wrong person was in the therapy room. She laughed and left my office smiling.

Is this based on correct information?

When addressing shame, it's important to question the information you have or the opinion you are given; is the "information" actually information, or is it an opinion from someone who doesn't have the right information themselves? Is it a valid source? Think back to the concept of erotic plasticity; much of our sexual shame is deeply embedded in everyone's history, mostly based on misguided opinions, fear and missing information. Remember, most women are not aware that their clitoris has eight thousand pleasure nerves, that sexual fantasies are normal, that women are inherently sensual and erotic, and that female sexuality and pleasure is only just being understood and researched.

As we have taken this journey together through this book, you may have gained new information and understanding, you might be starting to think about many aspects of your sexual self and your sexual pleasure more positively. You may want to ask yourself if some of your beliefs are still the same and if not, how are they different? What does that mean for you in the future? Exciting, isn't it!

Sammi was an online client from Canada - she was having problems with her arousal when with her partner. She told me, "I just can't get there, it's hopeless, this is so frustrating for my partner."

I asked her if it was frustrating for *her*? "Yes, because it's so disappointing for him, he feels like he failed."

I asked her to talk me through what happens. "We kiss for a while, he will touch my breasts and then my clit, then when I'm wet enough or we use lube we go for it, but I just can't get there."

I asked her about her pleasure. "I try really hard, we do all the right things, but I just can't get there."

I asked her, how do you know you are doing all the right things for *you*?

"Well, from porn and my friends, we follow the right pattern, but I just can't get there," she replied as she hunched over, looking deflated. I showed her the life size model of the clitoris and explained how amazing it was. She looked on in wonder as I held it up to the video camera and held my hand up next to it so she could get an idea of its size. In disbelief she questioned, "Eight thousand nerve endings, really? Wow that's really big!"

I told her, "Sammi, your clitoris, my clitoris, every woman's clitoris isn't the source of our sexual pleasure, it's the place where it accumulates and intensifies until we release it. Our arousal starts in our minds, our arousal is fed from every sense of our body, and our feelings and thoughts. If we see our arousal as something to work hard at, always thinking about the next step or the end point, we are never truly present in our arousal and appreciating the joy of just being in a glorious state of pleasure. We become preoccupied with what *should* come next, rather than what's happening now."

She sat back, looking thoughtful. "Hmmm, but that's not what happens in porn."

I smiled and nodded. "You're right - on the whole it isn't, but here's the reality: porn isn't real, it's a film like any other. The actors are acting

117

and usually, the target audience is men. Porn isn't a how-to-have-sex guide, just as the film *Independence Day* isn't a guide on how to beat an alien invasion; it's made up".

"Most women don't look like porn stars and our sexual arousal and responses don't manifest as they do in porn, it's just a fantasy, we often feel inadequate and full of shame because we don't match something that isn't real. It's because on the whole we are not given the information we are talking about now, and neither are our partners. I see a lot of men worried that they don't match up to the porn ideal, too."

"Oh my God," she said, "it's obvious when you sit back and think, how do I get rid of this shit? Let's get started."

Are my beliefs and opinions based on myths, fear or fact?

This is an important question to ask, am I worried what others might think? If so, why? Is my opinion based on fact or is it based on a myth? Myths about sexuality and sexual pleasure are still widely held as fact in society, most of them causing women to feel shame about parts of them that are completely the norm and natural. But when we take time to step back and question the myths, it becomes obvious that they hold very little, if any truth. Here are some of the common ones I encounter.

☐ **Being comfortable in our sexuality or sensuality is dangerous**. This myth stems from a time when it was believed that women could not control their sexual urges and needed to be controlled. Or that if we are comfortable in our sexuality and sexual pleasure, this would put us at risk for being sexually assaulted. That somehow our minds would be read and we would invite unwanted attention. But the exact opposite is true. If we have the right information, understand our bodies and are comfortable within our sexual pleasure, this means that we understand what we want and what we don't - we can give or deny consent. My definition of sexual freedom is the ability to choose to have a fulfilling and satisfying sex life in the absence of sexual dysfunction, guilt and shame. The key word being *choose*, if you are comfortable in your sexuality, you can make better choices that are right for you. Women that are comfortable sexually tend to be more confident and have healthy boundaries that protect them. It's safer to be sexually confident.

- **Women are less sexual than men.** This just isn't true, although we can have different triggers for arousal. Remember our higher level of erotic plasticity? Throughout our recent history we have been more repressed than men sexually by society. Thankfully, the understanding that women are equally sexual as men is now being accepted by society.

- **Women that have had several sexual partners have slack vaginas.** This myth is widely held, causing the slur "she's a bit loose", meaning careless or negligent. Here in northern England, the phrase "slack Alice" means a slovenly and slutty woman. But when we step back and ask ourselves what the likely difference in the elasticity of the vagina of a woman that has had sex with 100 people or the vagina of a woman that has had sex 100 times with the same person, the answer is none. It was a method to shame women and control them. Both women and men commonly have more than one sexual partner in their lifetime.

- **If you are comfortable sexually or like sex then you are a slut, a slapper or damaged goods.** Have you ever heard this said about a man? A male friend of mine once told me that he would do his best to have sex with a woman on a first date, and would always be disappointed if she did and he wouldn't see her again. I pointed out that meant he then must have also had sex on a first date, and he had a double standard going on. He was confused for a second and then the realisation hit him.

- **Women can't initiate sex**. Women can initiate sex, however we are taught that we shouldn't and that we are the gate keepers of sex. Most women were taught to fear sex as girls: *you might get pregnant,* *you will get a bad reputation, bad things will happen*, etc. We can and should be able to ask for what we need, and we also need to hear and respect a "no" response when it's given to us. There is no shame in asking for sex, or in being denied it.

☐ **Sex is a sin**. Sex is a joyous part of adult life, it is also essential to the survival of the human race. There is not a person on the planet who is here without it, even in the case of IVF, someone had an orgasm.

There are many more examples of sexual myths that are ingrained in society. We need to recognise them, question them and make them laughable nonsense that people used to believe.

Courage to challenge and change

Knowing you are experiencing misplaced shame is one thing, challenging it and changing how you feel about it is quite another. It takes courage to challenge shame, because often it means challenging things we have been taught, the people that taught it to us or the things that most people seem to believe. It can mean we have to digress from a current social norm, but we must also remember that as we do this, we are creating a new and informed one. Change can be uncomfortable, because with it comes the fear of uncertainty. To make changes we may have to redefine our boundaries, say "no" or say "yes" to things we never used to, change our course, have frank conversations and expand our thinking. It may mean we have to think or do things differently, and all of those things bring with it the fear of being judged negatively.

But here's the good news. Often, the thought of making a change is much worse than actually doing it. In fact, usually in the case of sexual shame, it is liberating, life changing and adds some serious heat to your lifeforce. When people challenge and change their own thinking and beliefs, the words they hear the most from people are, "I'm so grateful you expressed this", "Me too", "Thank you for your courage, because now I know I wasn't the only one and its inspired me to have courage, too".

Shame is so powerful because it isolates people. In reality, sexual shame is usually many people thinking and feeling the same thing but not talking about it, each thinking they are the only one and not realising they are one of many. Finding your courage breaks the disconnection shame creates, courage also leads to self-acceptance and self-compassion, it gives you permission to just be you.

"My definition of courage is never letting anyone define you."

- JENNA JAMESON

Let the past belief go

We all have a past; it doesn't define us. Your past beliefs, behaviour, successes and mistakes are all experiences that brought you to this very moment in time. Take the learnings and resources you need from that and let the past go. There may be things in your past you are not proud of. Guess what? Everyone has things in their past they are not proud of. Just let it go, don't hide from it, don't worry about what others might think if they find out. If someone tries to shame you for something in your past, look at them straight in the eye and say, "So what? We all have a past, even you."

Accept the new understanding

Having knowledge or evidence that your shame was misplaced is only part of the process; you must accept the new understanding. You need to walk your talk.

- ☐ Love your body, it's amazing (resources in Chapter 3).
- ☐ Luxuriate in your erotic bathtub (Chapter 2).
- ☐ Add heat to your lifeforce (Chapter 5).
- ☐ Embrace your eroticism (Chapter 7).
- ☐ Enforce your boundaries (Chapter 6).
- ☐ Have good consent practices (Chapter 6).
- ☐ Vocalise what you need and want (Chapter 6).
- ☐ Live your life sensually (Chapter 3).

121

Internalise

Because the original shame you felt was internalised, the change needs to be internalised too. Allow yourself to enjoy the feeling of embodying the new belief and understanding, notice how it feels and how wonderful the difference is. Notice your posture is prouder, your self-talk is positive, your confidence is more vibrant and celebrate all of that. Feel the change within you. Affirmations are a fantastic tool here; you need to say them with meaning and really feel them. You can also incorporate them into autogenic training. Examples of affirmations are:

- ☐ I am enough.
- ☐ I am sensual.
- ☐ I am comfortable in my sexual pleasure.
- ☐ I embrace my sexual arousal.
- ☐ I choose how I express my sexuality.
- ☐ I choose who I express my sexuality with.
- ☐ I am curious and loving about my body.
- ☐ I accept myself fully.
- ☐ I am unique.
- ☐ I trust myself.
- ☐ I deserve to experience pleasure.
- ☐ I live in possibility.

(Thank you to Mariana Matthews, AKA That Lady Hypnotist, for this last affirmation)

Move forward

Strive forward, seek out your sexual pleasure, be curious about it and embrace it when you find it. It's yours, you created it, share it with who you choose and how you choose.

Vulnerability – the frightened cousin of shame

Allowing yourself to be vulnerable is the most important aspect of a trusting intimate relationship with others and also within the relationship we have with yourself. Sometimes there are obstacles and blocks that prevent people from showing vulnerability and experiencing intimacy, such as the fear of being exposed or the fear of being be let down after being truly open. Many people are afraid to be vulnerable and question the shame they carry, to look closely at themselves and the opinions they have about themselves. We fear vulnerability because we are afraid that if someone finds out who we really are, they will reject us. While we may put on a front to protect us, trying to appear together, strong or intelligent in order to connect with others, it can actually cause the opposite: disconnection. It's exhausting.

A study by psychologist James Gross shows that when we are inauthentic and try to hide our feelings, others respond physiologically.[21] This physiological response may explain our discomfort or distrust around people we feel are not authentic. A study published by Katharina Kircanski, et al. [22] indicates that verbally expressing our feelings exactly as they are without beating around the bush may help us overcome emotions faster and communicate efficiently. When we allow ourselves to be completely open and vulnerable, the result is we benefit, our relationships improve, and we may even become more attractive to ourselves and others.

According to Dr. Brené Brown, in her TED talk *The Power of Vulnerability*, "Vulnerability is uncertainty, risk, and emotional exposure. Vulnerability is precisely 'sinking into' the joyful of moments in life. In other words, daring to show up and let ourselves to be seen."

[21] Gross, J. and Levenson, R., 1997. Hiding feelings: The acute effects of inhibiting negative and positive emotion. *Journal of Abnormal Psychology*, 106(1), pp.95-103.

[22] Kircanski, K., Lieberman, M. and Craske, M., 2012. Feelings Into Words. *Psychological Science*, 23(10), pp.1086-1091.

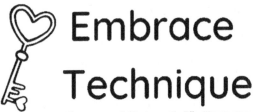

Embrace Technique

Resources available at www.KazRileyWoman.com

17.   *Healing your younger self*

Many of our views - both positive and negative - about our bodies, sex, sexuality and sexual pleasure are formed at a young age, often before we are aware what sex or sexual pleasure is. This process helps you to let go of the opinions and beliefs of others, misinformation and the shame that may have resulted. It also helps you to accept and integrate new knowledge and understanding, so that it becomes an embodied belief as you move forwards. If you have a lot of sexual trauma in your past, you might find it useful to have a therapist guide you through this process, all the therapists I have trained in this method can be found at: www.sexualfreedonhypnosis. org/findapractitioner.

- Imagine, see or just sense your psychological boundary (the one you created in Embrace Technique 13). Really allow yourself to experience the safety it brings you, within your boundary you are safe and free of judgement.

- Imagine on the outside of your boundary there is the future you; she has such a positive and confident presence. Know this is a version of you that has done all the work, made all the changes and embraced her sexuality and sexual pleasure fully and is released from any shame. Notice she has a playful glint in her eye and oozes sensuality. Her lifeforce is vibrant and strong.

- Invite your future self-inside your boundary, feel her presence intensify. Welcome her with an open heart. Imagine you can listen and learn from her; she has the knowledge and know-how. Listen as she tells you with love, that letting go of the weight of shame is easier than you might imagine. That it is a liberating and freeing experience. Know that she is there supporting you; she has your back, she is inside your boundary now and she is staying there. Feel the safety, love, relief, calm. Spend a while with these feelings.

- Notice on the outside of your boundary a younger version of yourself. Anytime since a moment ago is a younger version of you, it doesn't matter what age she is, she is just younger than you are now and whatever age your younger self is, is exactly the younger you that needs you right now.

- Notice how old she is, what she is wearing, the expression on her face and anything else you notice.

- Invite your younger self inside your boundary and welcome her with unconditional love. Tell her that she is in a safe, judgement free place and is protected.

- Ask the younger self to communicate with you, to express her fears and worries. Tell her you are listening, and she is being heard by you and your future self.

125

- Give your younger self the love and compassion she needs, reassure her, share your knowledge, allow her to be vulnerable in the safety of your boundary and know your future self is helping and guiding you as you do this.

- Give your younger self permission to let go of any shame and to embrace the parts of herself she felt shame about.

- Imagine a wonderful empowering group hug between you, your younger you and your future you. Imagine as you do this, they drift into you, the release and calm as the past is released and the new beliefs and knowledge is accepted on every level.

- Imagine yourself standing strong inside your boundary, feeling confident, sensual, at peace with yourself and comfortable with your sexuality and sexual pleasure, positive about moving forwards. Knowing you can live in possibility.

- Do this as many times as you need to with several versions of your younger self.

Resources available at www.KazRileyWoman.com

18.   *Mind your language*

Negative self-talk is something that most of us experience from time to time, and it comes in many forms. Negative self-talk can sound grounded and reasonable if we are not watching out for it. For example, "I'm not good at this, so don't do it", or "I can never do anything right!"

It may seem like a realistic appraisal of a situation: "This didn't lead to an orgasm. I guess I'm not good at sex", only to develop into a fear-based belief: "I will never have a good relationship".

Negative self-talk can sound a lot like a critical parent or friend from your past. It can catastrophise, blame, and shame you. Negative self-talk is any thought that diminishes your ability to make positive changes in your life or your confidence in yourself to do so. It can prevent your growth and ability to move forward. Negative self-talk can affect us in some damaging ways. One large-scale study found that rumination and self-blame over negative events were linked to an increased risk of mental health problems[23]. One of the most obvious drawbacks of negative self-talk is that it's not positive, research has shown that positive self-talk is a great predictor of success![24]

How to minimise negative self-talk

- ☐ **Catch yourself doing it.** Learn to notice when you're being self-critical so you can begin to stop. For example, notice when you say things to yourself that you wouldn't say to someone else.
- ☐ **Give your inner negative voice a nickname, a silly voice and externalise it.** When you think of your inner voice as a force outside of yourself and even give it a funny nickname and a silly voice, it becomes less threatening and easier to see how ridiculous some of your critical thoughts can be.
- ☐ **Contain your negativity.** It helps to contain the damage that a critical inner voice can cause by only allowing it to criticise certain things in your life, or be negative for only an hour in your day.

---

[23] Kinderman, P., Schwannauer, M., Pontin, E. and Tai, S., 2013. Psychological Processes Mediate the Impact of Familial Risk, Social Circumstances and Life Events on Mental Health. *PLoS ONE*, 8(10), p.e76564.

[24] Walter, N., Nikoleizig, L. and Alfermann, D., 2019. Effects of Self-Talk Training on Competitive Anxiety, Self-Efficacy, Volitional Skills, and Performance: An Intervention Study with Junior Sub-Elite Athletes. *Sports*, 7(6), p.148.

- **Cross-examine.** One of the damaging aspects of negative self-talk is that it often goes unchallenged. Challenge it! The vast majority of negative self-talk is an exaggeration, and calling yourself on this can help to take away its damaging influence.
- **Shift your perspective.** Imagine that you are looking at your problems from a great distance. Even thinking of the world as a globe and of yourself as a dot on it. This can often minimise the negativity, fear, and urgency in negative self-talk.
- **Replace the bad with some good.** Replace it with something better. Take a negative thought and change it to something encouraging that's also accurate.

Repeat until you find yourself needing to do it less and less often.

Resources available at www.KazRileyWoman.com

19.   *Autogenic training with a twist*

This autogenic training exercise can be used to help address stress, anxiety, fear, tension, etc... The more regularly it's used, the more powerful it becomes. Regular autogenic practice will help you feel more centred and more relaxed, calmer and quieter. It can help you embody new beliefs and connect those beliefs to feelings. Get into a comfortable position, take a deep breath and repeat each phrase quietly in your mind, slowly and rhythmically.

I am calm and relaxed.

My right arm is heavy. (Repeat 3 times).

128

My left arm is heavy. (Repeat 3 times).

My arms are heavy. (Repeat 3 times).

I am calm and relaxed.

My right leg is heavy. (Repeat 3 times).

My left leg is heavy. (Repeat 3 times).

My legs are heavy. (Repeat 3 times).

I am calm and relaxed.

My right hand is pleasantly warm. (Repeat 3 times).

My left hand is pleasantly warm. (Repeat 3 times).

My hands are pleasantly warm. (Repeat 3 times).

I am calm and relaxed.

My right foot is warm. (Repeat 3 times).

My left foot is warm. (Repeat 3 times).

My feet are pleasantly warm. (Repeat 3 times).

I am calm and relaxed.

My heartbeat is calm and regular. (Repeat 3 times).

My breathing is calm and regular. (Repeat 3 times).

My solar plexus is warm. (Repeat 3 times).

My forehead is cool. (Repeat 3 times).

I am very calm and relaxed. (Repeat 3 times).

I am enough. (Repeat 3 times).

I am a sensual woman. (Repeat 3 times).

I am comfortable in my sexual pleasure. (Repeat 3 times).

I embrace my sexual arousal. (Repeat 3 times).

I choose how I express my sexuality. (Repeat 3 times).

I choose who I express my sexuality with. (Repeat 3 times).

I am curious and loving about my body. (Repeat 3 times).

I accept myself fully. (Repeat 3 times).

I am unique. (Repeat 3 times).

I trust myself. (Repeat 3 times).

I deserve to experience pleasure. (Repeat 3 times).

I live in possibility. (Repeat 3 times).

You can add your own things in here, but make sure it is always a positive statement!

Resources for this chapter can be found at
www.kazrileywoman.com

CHAPTER NINE

Sexual function

If you are experiencing sexual problems, your doctor should be your first port of call. Sexual issues can be a symptom of physical disease that require the attention of your doctor. If you are concerned that a medication you are taking maybe causing a sexual issue, you should consult your doctor for advice.

Passion is the bridge that takes you from pain to change.

- FRIDA KAHLO

The study of female sexual function and dysfunction (FSD) is a relatively new science; it's only in the last twenty-five years that serious attention and focus has been given to understanding and treating the problems women have with sexual desire, arousal, pleasure and pain. In the year 2000, a new, more comprehensive model of female sexual dysfunction was proposed by a working group. Classifications were expanded to include psychogenic and organic causes of desire, arousal, orgasm and sexual pain disorders. An essential element of the new diagnostic system was personal distress. Over the last twenty years, there have been many studies across many countries looking at the prevalence of female sexual dysfunction (FSD) with partnered sex. The results are staggering.

Canada - 40%

Korea - 37%

Belgium[25] - 43.5%

Malaysia[26] - 25.8%

India[27] - 73.2%

USA - 43%

UK[28] - 15.5%

There are many more similar studies with very similar results. If we take an average of the seven countries listed above, 40% of women have a sexual dysfunction during partnered sex. But do they? As I stated at the beginning of this book, I am not a academic researcher or a medical doctor, I'm a therapist. But I find myself asking the question, how can something that happens to 40% of women be a dysfunction or abnormal?

In contrast, if you take the incidence of orgasm, just one of the aspects used to classify sexual dysfunction, and look at the difference in orgasmic capacity (always or usually reaching orgasm) in women during either partnered sex or whilst masturbating alone, the results are insightful. The Hite Report[29] - initially published in 1976 and updated in 2011

---

[25] Hendrickx, L., Gijs, L. and Enzlin, P., 2016. Sexual Difficulties and Associated Sexual Distress in Flanders (Belgium): A Representative Population-Based Survey Study. *The Journal of Sexual Medicine*, 13(4), pp.650-668.

[26] Ishak, I., Low, W. and Othman, S., 2010. Prevalence, Risk Factors, and Predictors of Female Sexual Dysfunction in a Primary Care Setting: A Survey Finding. *The Journal of Sexual Medicine*, 7(9), pp.3080-3087.

[27] Singh, J., Tharyan, P., Kekre, N., Singh, G. and Gopalakrishnan, G., 2009. Prevalence and risk factors for female sexual dysfunction in women attending a medical clinic in south India. *Journal of Postgraduate Medicine*, 55(2), p.113.

[28] Burri, A. and Spector, T., 2011. Recent and Lifelong Sexual Dysfunction in a Female UK Population Sample: Prevalence and Risk Factors. *The Journal of Sexual Medicine*, 8(9), pp.2420-2430.

[29] Hite, S., 2004. *The Hite Report: A Nationwide Study of Female Sexuality*. New York: Seven Stories Press.

- found that in a sample of 100,000 women, 95% of women could orgasm whilst masturbating, 85% of women having sex with women could orgasm, and 65% of women having sex with men could orgasm. So we know that women when masturbating have the same orgasmic capacity as men (95%), but when those same women are having sex with men, their orgasmic capacity falls by 30%. Men's orgasmic capacity didn't alter between partnered sex or masturbation. So if it's a norm that 40% of women experience problems with partnered sex, but not alone, then perhaps we need to ask the question, why is that?

Instead of labelling women as having a dysfunction, we need to understand what's going wrong with sex between men and women. Perhaps sexual dysfunction is not a *you have it or don't have it* thing, but something that is on a spectrum, impacting women on different levels, in different situations, and with different partners.

Much of the recent research has been funded by pharmaceutical companies looking to find the female equivalent to Pfizer's diamond-shaped wonder drug for erectile dysfunction - Viagra. This fact was highlighted in an article published in the British Medical Journal, "The making of a disease: female sexual dysfunction"[30] that raised concerns about how research was being carried out and by whom. The article asked the question "Is a new disorder being identified to meet unmet needs or to build markets for new medications?" As part of the article, Dr John Bancroft, the director of the Kinsey Institute at Indiana University, states that he believes the term 'dysfunction' is highly misleading, and he is one of several researchers critical of the corporate-sponsored definitions. He argues that an inhibition of sexual desire is in many situations a healthy and functional response for women faced with stress, tiredness, or threatening patterns of behaviour from their partners. "The danger of portraying sexual difficulties as a dysfunction is that it is likely to encourage doctors to prescribe drugs to change sexual function—when

[30] Moynihan, R., 2003. The making of a disease: female sexual dysfunction. *BMJ*, 326(7379), pp.45-47.

133

the attention should be paid to other aspects of the woman's life. It's also likely to make women think they have a malfunction when they do not."

My personal opinion is that the answer to this question is both, we need a classification of female sexual dysfunction, but it also needs to recognise the causes of female sexual dysfunction many of which could never be solved by popping a pill. In reality, popping a pill like Viagra or something similar doesn't solve men's sexual issues either. It certainly helps men get and maintain erections, but my clinic is still full of men with sexual anxiety who use Viagra regularly. I also see many women who have very life-limiting sexual dysfunctions that stop them from having sex and relationships, but the physical aspect is only one part of it. Dr Sandra Leiblum, Professor of Psychiatry at Robert Wood Johnson Medical School and a clinical psychologist, believes real sexual dysfunction is much less prevalent than 40%. The figure has contributed to an over medicalisation of women's sexuality, changes in sexual desire are the norm. "I think there is dissatisfaction and perhaps disinterest among a lot of women, but that doesn't mean they have a disease," she said during an interview at the New York educational workshop. So as we move forward with this chapter on sexual dysfunctions I invite you to think about them as a **difficulty** rather than a dysfunction, disorder or disease.

What are the most common sexual difficulties?

Reduced libido/sex drive

Most women experience a temporary reduction in sexual desire and/or arousal at some point in their lives. This is both common and normal during or after pregnancy, or at times of stress. However, if these symptoms persist, are present all or most of the time, and cause you distress, then you should see your doctor to rule out an underlying physical cause. A loss of libido can have a range of physical or psychological causes, including:

→ **Trauma.** You may find one to one sessions with a therapist helpful to address this. www.sexualfreedomhypnosis.com/findapractitioner.

→ **Tiredness.** Enough sleep is essential to every function of your body and mind, especially your libido/lifeforce.

→ **Diabetes.** Both Type 1 and Type 2 diabetes.

→ **Hormone disorders and/or imbalance**. Thyroid issues, perimenopause, menopause- your doctor can check for these issues.

→ **Excessive alcohol consumption or drug use.** It is very difficult to have a strong lifeforce in the grips of a substance dependency or addiction.

→ **SSRI type of antidepressants.** Do not stop taking any medication, consult with your doctor about any changes that need to me made. Problems with libido and/or orgasm are well-known side effects of SSRI antidepressants;[31] sometimes the underlying depression is blamed for this side effect.

→ **Contraceptive medication. The pill, implants and Mirena coil.** Do not stop taking any medication, consult with your doctor about any changes that need to me made.

→ **Shame** (Chapter 8).

→ **Lost eroticism** (Chapter 7).

→ **Orgasm focused sex** (Chapter 7).

→ **Lost sensuality** (Chapter 3).

→ **Sexual performance anxiety.**

→ **Body confidence issues** (Chapter 3).

→ **Relationship problems** (Chapters 3,6,7,8).

→ **Depression and anxiety** (Chapter 6).

→ **Low self-esteem** (Chapter 6).

→ **Inability to accept and receive pleasure** (Chapters 3,5,6,10,11,15).

---

[31] E. Fooladi, R. J. Bell & S. R. Davis (2012) Management strategies in SSRI-associated sexual dysfunction in women at midlife, Climacteric, 15:4, 306-316

Libido is your lifeforce (Chapter 5). Because your lifeforce is a vital part of who you are, how you view the world and how you experience sexual pleasure, it needs work, care and maintenance. In my therapy room, I see many women with libido issues. They are often full of fear that their partner will be forced to go outside of the relationship for sex. Many report that they will have sex to please their partner, meaning that often they are enduring sex rather than enjoying it (which will reinforce a negative influence on libido). Lifeforce or lack of it is closely linked to our ability to experience sexual pleasure, how we feel about ourselves influences how worthy we feel. It makes sense that if we have anxiety about sex, our sexual performance, our bodies or shame about our sexual pleasure, that the result will be a decreased desire. Libido/lifeforce is a multi-faceted complex part of us that we need to nurture. It relies upon our erotic bathtubs being filled (Chapter 2), good health, enough sleep, feeling connected to yourself, and many other things.

Dyspareunia (painful sex)

This is a persistent or recurrent pain that can happen during sex. The defining symptom of dyspareunia is pain with intercourse that may occur at the vaginal opening or deep in the pelvis. The pain may be distinct and localised, or there may be a broader sense of discomfort. There may be an aching, burning, throbbing, or ripping sensation. Dissatisfaction with, or disinterest in, sex and physical intimacy can result. Pain always needs investigating by a doctor to determine the cause. Causes of painful sex include:

Physical

→ Genital injury
→ Postpartum dyspareunia (pain after childbirth)
→ Inflammation or infection
→ Vaginal yeast infections

→ Urinary tract infections

→ Sexually transmitted infections

→ Skin disorders or irritation

→ Irritation or allergic reactions

→ Pelvic surgery

→ Cystitis

→ Endometriosis (growth of the lining of the womb in other areas of the body)

→ Fibroids

→ Ovarian cysts

→ Uterine prolapse

→ Sexual position (some women experience pain in certain sexual positions, find the ones that are comfortable)

→ Hormone imbalances

→ Irritable bowel syndrome (the most common cause of IBS is internalised anxiety; hypnotherapy is a recommended treatment option by the national institute of clinical excellence (NICE) in the UK)

Psychological

→ Anxiety

→ Fear of pain

→ Depression

→ Stress

→ Guilt or shame about sex

→ Lack of arousal

Painful sex and/or vaginismus is the third most common sexual problem women seek help for at my clinic. Physical sexual pain is significantly under-reported, partly because many women are taught that sex hurts when they are younger, so they put up with it or they are too embarrassed to talk to a doctor about it.

Many of the women I work with have experienced sexual pain for years. A large component of sexual pain and vaginismus is a pain cycle known as the fear, tension, pain cycle.

The fear tension pain cycle was first documented in a book titled *Childbirth Without Fear* by a doctor called Grantley Dick-Read. He suggested that fear causes a woman to become tense, and that tension increases pain. The increased pain, in turn, increases fear, and the cycle repeats. Dick-Read noticed that the more fear a labouring woman had, the more tension she holds in her body, the more her pain increases, leading to more fear. He also found that if this cycle could be broken, women had much more comfortable birth experiences. This principle has been used to aid women in labour via hypnosis for birth techniques for decades.

The same principle can be applied to sexual pain; it makes sense that if you know something may be painful or fear that it might be, your body will tense as a result, leading to pain or an increase of it. Fear also produces adrenaline that triggers the fight or flight response. This response dampens the production of sex hormones needed for arousal and triggers feelings of anxiety, not helpful in intimate or sexual situations that are consensual and safe. The fight/flight response also influences blood flow in the body. The blood flow is increased to the body parts needed to fight or run away (heart, lungs, limbs) and is decreased to the ones needed the least (sexual organs and the digestive system). This means that a woman in the grips of this response during a sexual situation can experience fear, pain, decrease in arousal, reduced blood flow to the vulva and clitoris, shifts into thinking mode from feeling mode causing a disconnection from the experience and the woman looking for or waiting for pain.

This cycle can be halted in two ways:

Reduce fear

→ Getting checked over by your doctor can help you understand the cause of the pain or know there is no physical cause of pain that needs medical attention.

→ Having good knowledge about how your body works and responds sexually is key to overcoming sexual pain (Chapter 3).

→ Self-exploration and masturbation help you understand how your body feels and responds at various levels and stages of arousal (Chapters 3, 10).

→ Having excellent consent practices and boundaries helps you feel in control and safe. Safe words are useful here! (Chapter 6).

→ Being open and honest with a partner about the issue, it is nothing to be ashamed of (Chapter 6).

→ Healing the younger self to let go of any negative past experiences or faulty beliefs about sex (Chapter 8).

Reduce tension

→ Respect your yes and no responses (Chapter 6).

→ Allow your arousal to build, focus on sensuality, connection and pleasure, and luxuriate within it for a prolonged period of time (Chapters 3,5,7,10,11).

→ Give yourself time and wait until you are aching and craving for genital or clitoral touch for a short while before doing or permitting that.

→ Only move towards penetration when you feel so aroused that you are almost feeling a desperation to be penetrated, that the act of being penetrated will bring relief rather than pain.

→ Learn how to relax rather than try, add in the phrase "my body is comfortable when aroused" or "penetration is relief" into your autogenic training practice (Chapter 8).

One of the biggest blocks to overcoming sexual pain is the fear of disappointing or upsetting a partner.

"It will be frustrating for him if we have to stop, so I just don't do it in the first place".

"He would be devastated if he thought sex was hurting me, so I just don't tell him" are phrases I hear often from clients. This means that many women see their partner's experiences as far more important than their own sexual satisfaction, comfort, and pleasure. Long term, this is detrimental to desire, lifeforce and connection in relationships. When women communicate with a partner about the pain they are experiencing, most just want to help and are more than happy to explore, slow down or stop when needed and just support their partner as the issue is worked through.

Embrace Technique

Resources available at www.KazRileyWoman.com

20. *Freddy Jacquin's Arrow Technique*

Pain is a subjective experience that normally feels unpleasant, like something in the body has been, or is being damaged or destroyed; that feels like a threat to or interference with one's ongoing functionality and health; and that is associated with negative emotions, such as fear, anxiety, anger or depression. The Arrow Technique places importance on the subjective 'felt experience' of the person in pain. Pain has a sensory and an emotional component. These two components are often intertwined. One of the keys to relieving pain is to disentangle these two components, the sensory and physical, from the emotional and mental. Without the emotional element, what pain is left does not hurt as much or at all.

- Sitting comfortably, focus on your breathing. Pretend and imagine that you are breathing in calmness and breathing out tension. And as you continue to breathe like this, just focus on your body and if you notice any tension anywhere just let it go as you exhale.

- In your mind softly and slowly repeat the word **relax** four times. As you repeat that word you can begin to relax. Let every muscle relax. As you do that, you may become more aware of the ideas and images, that drift into the mind automatically. Allow yourself to drift down deeper and deeper into that feeling. Allow yourself to drift deeper and deeper, and imagine that it is happening all by itself.

- Allow yourself to have the experience of drifting up out of your body; drift away from your body and drift way, way up above your body, hundreds, thousands of feet above your body, leaving all physical ties behind, floating all the way up.

- Notice how it feels to be up there and as you look around, notice the variety of things that compete for your attention. Now in your mind's eye, look down, and way, way down below you'll see a target, like an archery target. See that target clearly in your mind; see the coloured bands, see the bullseye; now in that bullseye is the pain you were experiencing.

- Now imagine you could be fired like an arrow, straight at that bullseye, and go straight right through that bullseye into a place of no pain. As you pass through the bullseye, you will experience that pain intensify for a split-second and then drift into a place where you are completely free of that and feelings of freedom, love and self-acceptance are waiting for you.

- Be brave about this. So know in a moment you will be shot like an arrow straight through that target, so get ready.

- Go, you are an arrow going straight through the bulls eye on the target. Pass through it and out the other side. Into a place of no pain, calm open, awareness, just drifting in a place completely free of any unnecessary pain, drifting as a mind, free of all earthly ties, free of all distractions. You drift there, in that beautiful feeling of open awareness, completely free of any unnecessary pain or discomfort.

- Now imagine you can drift to the other side of the room that you are sitting in, drift to the other side of the room you're sitting in and from there see yourself sitting in that chair, you can see yourself sitting in that chair.

- Notice that from the other side of the room as you watch yourself sitting in that chair, that every ounce of agitation and unnecessary pain has gone from your body and those thoughts have left your mind. You cannot experience them, you cannot feel any pain, you are completely separated from your body, and as you drift there, completely free.

- In a while you are going to drift back over to your body, but only as quickly as your body and mind can make all the changes that will allow you that freedom, the freedom to experience freedom from any unnecessary pain any time you wish to or need to. Only then will you drift back over to your body and drop down into your body, free of agitation, free of distractions. Take your time, as you are aware of the images and the sounds as you drift over, back into your body, unable to experience those old feelings. Go ahead, take your time. When you are fully reintegrated, get on with your day, taking that comfort with you.

Vaginal dryness

Vaginal dryness (not getting wet enough for comfortable penetration) can be a cause of great concern, shame and pain for women. Wetness is a physical marker of sexual arousal and one that a partner will often look for and comment on. "Wow, you are so wet!"

"You're not wet, is something wrong, are you not enjoying this?"

"Are you wet enough yet?"

Vaginal dryness can be caused by physical, hormonal and psychological problems.

Causes of vaginal dryness:

→ **Reduction in oestrogen**, particularly after menopause or childbirth. Your doctor can help you.

→ **Antidepressants.** Do not stop taking any medication, consult with your doctor about any changes that need to me made.

→ **Antihistamines.** Do not stop taking any medication, consult with your doctor about any changes that need to me made.

→ **Contraceptive medication**. Do not stop taking any medication, consult with your doctor about any changes that need to be made.
→ **Damage to the Bartholin's glands.**
→ **Inadequate foreplay.**
→ **Anxiety.**

It's effortless to reach for the lube or coconut oil to solve this problem. In some cases where arousal is high, the desire to be penetrated is overwhelming and little or no natural lubrication has occurred, then by all means grab the lube and enjoy yourself. But in the cases where there simply hasn't been enough foreplay (or core-play as we will define in Chapter 11) or anxiety is present, it's much more likely that your body simply isn't ready for penetration. Learn to GLIDE before breaking out the lube. It really isn't a case of being "wet enough" for penetration, it's about feeling you absolutely need and want to be penetrated, right now!

Learn to GLIDE

GLIDE into Arousal

→ Give yourself permission to receive pleasure.
→ Luxuriate in your arousal.
→ Ignore time.
→ Desire to be penetrated is overwhelming.
→ Ease up and slow down.

Then, if needed, use the lube.

Vaginismus

The involuntary contraction of the pelvic floor muscles causes vaginismus, leading to painful sexual intercourse or preventing penetration altogether. This can happen as the partner attempts penetration, when a woman inserts a tampon, and/or when a woman is touched near the vaginal area. Vaginismus usually doesn't interfere with sexual arousal, but it can prevent penetration and cause problems with libido. A gentle pelvic exam by a doctor typically shows no cause of the contractions. No physical abnormalities contribute to the condition, although vaginismus can be caused by an allergy to latex condoms in rare cases. Vaginismus effects around 17% of women.[32]

Causes of vaginismus:

→ Lack of body knowledge.

→ Fear of pregnancy.

→ Fear of pain.

→ Conditioned body response.

→ Belief systems.

→ Shame.

→ Negative past sexual experience.

→ Exposure to pornography. Much of the portrayal of penetrative sex in pornography is of rough sex, little foreplay and women having very little control. The Male actors in pornography also have a gigantic penis size, which to many women looks painful. The result is a protective movement to prevent damage, probably a similar mind body response to a man instinctively reaching down to cover his testicles when only witnessing another man being "kicked in the balls".

---

[32] Pacik, P., 2014. Understanding and treating vaginismus: a multimodal approach. *International Urogynecology Journal*, 25(12), pp.1613-1620.

The treatment for vaginismus is a combination of vaginal dilators, pelvic floor exercises and talking therapy such as hypnotherapy. There is a huge mind component to overcoming vaginismus. To quote my client in a recent interview on my YouTube channel *Trancing in the Sheets*, "It's all about mind set and understanding my body. We are not taught about our bodies in school. Once I changed my mindset I became free and now I feel like a Woman for the first time."

Case study

Sally, 34, was a graphic designer who contacted me after her recent divorce. She had vaginismus since trying to use a tampon aged 15 and was not able to be penetrated with a finger or tampon. She had a healthy libido, could orgasm through clitoral stimulation and had enjoyed lots of intimacy in the past with her now ex-partner. She was functioning normally sexually with the exception of being penetrated. She had no past history of abuse and described her upbringing as a happy one. She had seen a psychosexual therapist in the past and had been given relaxation exercises and a set of vaginal dilators, which hadn't been successful. Sally told me that she had tried to relax, but as soon as she had tried to use the dilators, she felt anxious and tense. Sally was now ready after her recent divorce to start dating, but felt that a new partner might not be as understanding as her ex-husband, she felt that she couldn't start dating until she had overcome her vaginismus. Over a period of five weeks, Sally attended three sessions with me, each lasting eighty minutes.

Session one: boundaries

Sally's boundaries were very porous, she was a life-long people pleaser and that often caused her anxiety. After gently guiding her into hypnosis we tightened up her boundaries, amplified her yes and no's, gave her permission to enforce them and brought her newly learned knowledge about her body inside her boundary. She felt very calm after the session. I set her homework that focused on autogenic training and to listen to a download in order to reinforce her improved boundary.

Session two: healing the younger self

Sally arrived for a second session and told me she had felt much calmer during the last ten days, she was also amused that every time she had felt stressed she had heard my voice in the background asking, "inside or outside your boundary?"

Using hypnosis I guided Sally back to her boundary, we checked that they were strong, and she felt secure. Sally described her future self as a bit *kick ass* – smiling, she said, "Wow, I've totally got my shit together."

We turned our attention to a younger version of her, the younger self that was needing to be heard. A fourteen-year-old Sally appeared at her boundary. Sally described the younger her looking worried and upset. I asked her to listen and find out what was wrong, to communicate with and reassure the younger Sally. After a while I guided Sally to tell me what her younger self needed, she said, "I was watching TV with my dad and he had asked if I had a boyfriend, so I told him I did." He had looked at her and said, "Do not open your legs, you must always keep them closed, you know what I mean?"

"So what does she need to know?" I asked.

Sally smiled and said, "That when the time is right you can open your legs and that's OK."

Later in the session I asked Sally to notice that she could open her legs, she was safe in my office, fully clothed and under a blanket, that the motion of spreading her legs would feel incredible and freeing, a wonderful empowering trigger for calm relaxation. We did this several times and each time she relaxed more. I set a post hypnotic suggestion for her, that the next time she was fantasising and masturbating, she would feel an urge to open her legs. She would feel safe and it would feel good to explore her labia, vulva and clitoris. That doing this would feel wonderful and she would simply do what felt good to her, in her own time and in her own way. I closed the session and asked her to carry on with the autogenic training, adding the phrase *It feels good to open my legs*. Three days later I got a text from Sally that said, "Sorry if this is TMI, but I had to tell you, I just fingered myself and it felt amazing."

Session three: accepting

A few weeks later Sally had her third session, she had used a tampon for the first time and had met a man via a dating site and had been on a couple of dates. She was excited about the possibility of having sex at some point in the future and was feeling much more relaxed generally. During the hypnosis part of her session, we checked in on her younger self who was smiling and happy. We directed her breath down into her abdomen filling her body with a warm welcoming sensation. We moved the breath downward until she could imagine that she could breathe in and out through her vaginal opening – this is also known as "Yoni Breathing", which involves imagining that each muscle would relax and open when the time was right. I asked Sally to imagine that she could feel her vaginal opening filling with light, gradually getting wider until it was as open as it would ever need to be, that she could confirm this later at home with her dilators and that it would feel good to do so. We closed the session and I asked her to practice the yoni breathing at home.

Two months later I received a text from Sally that said "I opened my legs; I had sex and I didn't hurt! I really don't understand why I couldn't (before). Thank you, can you help with fear of flying?"

When pain is there to stay

In most cases of sexual pain, the pain can be reduced or eliminated. But there are cases where it cannot be, or that penetration would cause damage to the vaginal canal. In those situations a woman can still find and embrace her sexual pleasure. Penetration is only one part of sex; it is not the goal of sex and as we've discussed throughout this book, our sexuality and sensuality are much more than physical acts. Women who find penetration too painful can still experience high levels of arousal and orgasmic bliss; they can do this alone or with a partner and both parties still come away feeling deeply connected and satisfied.

Anorgasmia

This is the inability to achieve orgasm, despite sufficient sexual stimulation and is associated with personal distress. The inability to orgasm only qualifies as anorgasmia if it's accompanied by feelings of:

→ Frustration
→ Self-doubt
→ Shame
→ Inadequacy
→ Anger

Primary anorgasmia/ lifelong anorgasmia is never having an orgasm, even after "sufficient" stimulation. Primary anorgasmia is most common in people who:

→ Are younger
→ Are less sexually experienced
→ Grew up in sexually repressive environments
→ Self-conscious

Secondary anorgasmia means a person has previously orgasmed, but over time orgasmic response has disappeared or has greatly reduced. Secondary anorgasmia is most common in people who:

→ Have had genital surgery
→ Recently gave birth or experienced menopause
→ Were assaulted
→ Recently started a new medication
→ Have experienced a change in weight
→ Have recently been injured
→ Are in a new relationship

Situational anorgasmia occurs when you aren't able to orgasm during certain sexual activities or situations. This can be a very misleading term because it can be applied to situations or activities during which most women wouldn't orgasm. For example, it's **very** common to not orgasm during sexual activities that don't provide the type of stimulation you need to orgasm. Less than 20% of women can orgasm from penetration alone[33], which would pathologicalise the 80% of women who don't orgasm during sex with no clitoral stimulation.

Anorgasmia and/or libido issues are the main reasons my clients contact me for help, the whole of the next chapter is devoted to orgasmic bliss!

---

[33] Herbenick, D., Fu, T., Arter, J., Sanders, S. and Dodge, B., 2017. Women's Experiences With Genital Touching, Sexual Pleasure, and Orgasm: Results From a U.S. Probability Sample of Women Ages 18 to 94. *Journal of Sex & Marital Therapy*, 44(2), pp.201-212.

CHAPTER TEN

The hot pursuit of the big 'O' (Part One)

"*Electric flesh-arrows ... traversing the body. A rainbow of colour strikes the eyelids. A foam of music falls over the ears. It is the gong of the orgasm.*"

- ANAÏS NIN, *THE DIARY OF ANAÏS NIN*

Often described as a powerful, pleasurable release of accumulated sexual tension, the orgasm is perceived as the epitome of sexual pleasure for both men and women.

During orgasm, you may experience a rise in blood pressure, an increased heart rate, heavy breathing, and rhythmic muscular contractions.

If we believe the portrayal of the female orgasm in films, books and pornography, it doesn't take much for a woman to cum. According to these 'sources', a woman can happily sit having a cup of tea thinking about what she might have for lunch, and when suddenly she sees a man she finds attractive, they kiss, and high levels of arousal surge through her body from nowhere, flicked on like a switch and turned up to intense, overwhelming levels of desire and want in just a few minutes. Then, she is ready; ready to be penetrated, and in almost an instant, the orgasms take over.

Gigantic, screaming, shaking orgasms that take her to another realm all in the space of five minutes, less than the time it took her to make the tea she was drinking in the first place. Even portrayals that depict prolonged sexual encounters, on the whole, follow a similar pattern, and the focus is on penetration in every imaginable sexual position. The inference of this is that heteronormative sex is focused on penetration, that orgasms will be the result of that, and arousal is a quick to occur process, with the sole purpose of becoming ready for penetration. The real-life facts and experience bare minimal resemblance to this, but for many, it creates an expectation of how becoming orgasmic should be, rather than how it actually is. This takes away from the experience of sexual pleasure both when alone or with another or others.

Simply put, it's the equivalent to believing you can fly through the air like Supergirl because a film told you that you could. In Chapter Seven, we looked at how fantasy fuels our eroticism and sexual pleasure; fantasy is an essential part of the "Mind" aspect of our sexual pleasure and will help you access it more easily. But we must also remember that our fantasies or the ones shown to us in films or pornography are not a "How to" or "It works this way" guide to arousal, sex, sexual pleasure and orgasm. They are just fantasies.

Orgasm is a beautiful experience for most people, but not everyone. Some women refer to the sensation of orgasm as being a frightening experience, others describe it as being the most exciting, fulfilling, and enjoyable sensation imaginable[34]. Some women fear the experience of orgasm, see it as the ultimate loss of control and consider it to be a vulnerability that should be avoided.[35] In my therapy office, I see many

---

[34] Blackledge, C., 2004. *The story of V*. New Brunswick, N.J.: Rutgers University Press.

[35] Laan, E. and Rellini, A., 2011. Can we treat anorgasmia in women? The challenge to experiencing pleasure. *Sexual and Relationship Therapy*, 26(4), pp. 329-341.

women who have difficulties reaching orgasm. How this presents and what it means differs significantly from woman to woman.

Quotes from intake forms and consultations with women with anorgasmia:

- ♀ "My partner does not do enough foreplay, but I want to be able to orgasm just with penetration."
- ♀ "I have never had difficulty achieving orgasm through masturbation (although recently I have, as I have been feeling really stressed and can't concentrate well, even when alone!) With a partner I feel very self-conscious, performative and ashamed of my pleasure. I have a fear of letting go in front of another person. It feels like I am giving them some sort of power over me which feels very scary."
- ♀ "I have never found orgasms with a partner easy. My mind is not quiet during sex - often thinking about my body, and the fact I can't orgasm even though I'm finding it pleasurable. Even during oral sex that I love and get good sensations from, I can't orgasm."
- ♀ "Difficulty achieving orgasm (if ever)/low sexual arousal. Impacting marriage as it is, affecting my husband's sense of self-esteem. I am afraid he's going to leave me if I can't overcome this. It's not his fault, he has never had this problem in previous relationships."
- ♀ "I cannot orgasm in the presence of a partner, I can nearly get there with oral sex, and then nothing happens, it's like my body is stuck."
- ♀ "Aim to orgasm with my partner every time - whether it's a quickie or longer session where I'd like a variety of orgasms perhaps several and squirting on occasion."
- ♀ I enjoy sex/lovemaking but am frustrated that I cannot orgasm. I can orgasm by myself. I am self-conscious about my body. I can't walk around or even stand naked."
- ♀ "Trying to orgasm and worrying that I can't - knowing that my partner knows I'm not; I'm annoyed that I can't."

♀ "My orgasms are weak, there is this huge build up and then a tingle, it's really not worth the effort."

♀ "I have orgasmed once using a vibrator, that is the only time I can recall."

♀ "I was brought up in a very religious environment, I have left all that behind, but I think it may have something to do with my inability to orgasm, when I self-pleasure it feels like I shouldn't be doing that, and I stop."

♀ "When I orgasm I feel overwhelmed with emotion and cry, I fear this feeling."

♀ "I had an abortion four years ago; I have not orgasmed since."

♀ "I am making my partner feel inadequate sexually, when I don't cum he blames himself and I feel awful."

♀ "I feel the contractions of an orgasm in my body, but I feel no pleasure."

♀ "I don't think I've ever gotten near to climaxing, all the right things are happening, and nothing happens."

My approach to working with women who have orgasm issues depends on what the difficulty is; how it is presenting; and in what circumstances. If a woman has never been able to orgasm in any circumstances, has very weak orgasms or has had a recent change in her orgasmic capacity, and if she hasn't been checked over by her doctor recently or had her oestrogen and testosterone levels evaluated, the first thing I recommend is a visit to the doctor's office. Once the client has the-all clear from her doctor, we start myth busting.

Orgasm myths

The myths surrounding the female orgasm are as numerous as those surrounding sex.

Women find reaching orgasm harder than men do, studies now prove this myth to be untrue. What is true is that women have a much harder time reaching orgasm through penetration with a man, or during sexual intimacy with a man than they do when having sex with another woman or when masturbating. In a 2018 study of 52,588 Americans[36], the orgasmic capacity (the ability to orgasm) was found to be 95% for both men and women when they were masturbating. The results changed when the study looked at sexual intimacy. When the parameter "usually or always orgasmed when sexually intimate" was analysed, the results are fascinating. The term "sexually intimate" means a sexual experience, as a woman might have orgasmed during the period of being intimate, but not necessarily during penetration. The results for orgasm through penetration is given as a separate figure.

o Heterosexual men - the figure remained at 95%
o Gay men - 89%
o Bisexual men - 88%
o Lesbian women - 86%
o Bisexual women - 66%
o Heterosexual women - 65%
  (during sexual intimacy)

In another 2018 study of 1,055 women[37]:

o 18.4% of women reported that intercourse alone was sufficient for orgasm.
o 36.6% reported clitoral stimulation was necessary for orgasm during penetrative sex.

[36] Frederick, D., John, H., Garcia, J. and Lloyd, E., 2017. Differences in Orgasm Frequency Among Gay, Lesbian, Bisexual, and Heterosexual Men and Women in a U.S. National Sample. *Archives of Sexual Behavior*, 47(1), pp.273-288.

[37] Herbenick, D., Fu, T., Arter, J., Sanders, S. and Dodge, B., 2017. Women's Experiences With Genital Touching, Sexual Pleasure, and Orgasm: Results From a U.S. Probability Sample of Women Ages 18 to 94. *Journal of Sex & Marital Therapy*, 44(2), pp.201-212.

o 36% indicated that, while clitoral stimulation was not needed, their orgasms feel better if their clitoris is stimulated during intercourse.

So, this means in the general population, 95% of women have orgasmic capacity, but less than 20% of women achieve orgasm through penetration alone. In terms of sexual dysfunction, over 80% of women have the dysfunction termed "situational anorgasmia" when it comes to penetrative sex with men. Common sense tells us that if 80% of women experience the same thing, that must be the norm and cannot possibly be a dysfunction.

There are different types of orgasm - vaginal orgasm, clitoral orgasm and blended orgasm

This myth is a legacy left behind by Sigmund Freud. He believed that a clitoral orgasm was an immature version of a vaginal one, - he defined a vaginal orgasm as an orgasm that had occurred through penetration from a penis. Remember that Freud was also promoting the idea of female sexual hysteria as a mental illness; the symptoms of which were masturbation, sexual fantasies, women having sex with other women and a high libido. So he pathologicalised anything other than orgasm via penetration with a penis, simply because it didn't fit his theory. That orgasm through penile penetration was the only way a woman *should* orgasm, anything else was seen as lesser than or "immature", i.e. if you can't orgasm with a man, then there is something wrong with you. He also used fear to enforce his nonsense, if a woman didn't shift her focus from a clitoral orgasm to a vaginal one she was risking giving herself a psychological disorder.

Taking into account that at that time in history, the anatomy of the clitoris was not fully understood, what was understood was being actively ignored and the stigma and sometimes dire consequences of diagnosis of a mental disorder had at that time, you can see how Freud was able to convince people that there must be more than one kind of orgasm and that a vaginal orgasm was the goal of a well-balanced and respectable woman. Freud himself in later life stated that he was wrong and that we would be better served by listening to someone with better knowledge than him, but the misguided ideal of the vaginal orgasm still lives on today.

Orgasms can feel very different but all of them involve the clitoris. Your clitoris is the size of your palm, has internal and external parts and can be stimulated by thought alone, stimulation of another body part causing arousal and blood flow to the clitoris, direct stimulation of the clitoral glans (tip), rubbing of the whole vulva, and internal stimulation through the vaginal canal wall being pressed or rubbed with a tongue, finger, sex toy or penis. A blended orgasm is simply where there is a blend of stimulation to the clitoris, you could say that all orgasms are blended because the mind is a major part of every orgasm So the question is not what kind of orgasm can I have, but what stimulation do I need to reach orgasm?

Orgasms from penetrative sex are most common and the healthiest form of sexual expression

We have already busted the first part of this myth by understanding that less than 20% of women reach orgasm via penetrative sex, so an orgasm from penetrative sex are the least common. The "healthiest form of sexual expression"? I suspect that's a relic from the time that women's sexuality was much more controlled; and where we were told that only sex (orgasm) with a man was acceptable and anything else was shameful or less than.

Women need to be in love to orgasm

Another relic from the past, from the long-gone belief that only a woman in a committed relationship (marriage) should be having sex. This belief was also used to pressure women into sex - "If you loved me, you would,"

157

- which fuelled the idea that if you don't orgasm with a man you don't find him attractive or arousing.

A partner can tell if a woman has had an orgasm

There is only one way a partner can tell if a woman is having an orgasm or had one. She tells them. They might be obvious signs that she could be, but most women outwardly express their orgasms in very different ways.

All women express orgasmic pleasure in the same way

There is an expectation on how a woman should express her orgasm and/or arousal. This causes many women to "perform" their sexual arousal when with a partner, which can take away from her sexual pleasure. Pornography and depictions of sex teaches us that we should be screaming as orgasmic bliss sweeps through us. For some women that is precisely how it occurs, others become very quiet as they experience an orgasm, and most women do different things at different times. There is no standard or right way of experiencing an orgasm.

Women who cannot orgasm have psychological problems

Trauma, performance anxiety, relationship issues, and poor mental health can make it more difficult for a woman to orgasm, but these things cause no problem for many women. Many people with healthy sexual attitudes and/or good relationships can still have difficulties. The ability to orgasm or not is not an indicator of a person's psychological health.

Squirting isn't authentic or squirting is an ideal

Squirting is very real. But it rarely looks like it does in pornography; the gushing seen in pornography films is performance (remember, porn isn't real). The squirting is often the product of water packets inserted into the vagina as a special effect to enhance the film. Squirting isn't a marker of a better or worse orgasm, some women squirt, some squirt sometimes and some never do. Squirting can also occur when a woman isn't orgasming. The perceived requirement to squirt during sex is a relatively new thing. This has mainly come about from its appearance in pornography, causing people to believe this is what an almighty orgasm looks like. So now many women are not only required to chase an orgasm but also squirt as well. Researchers still don't quite understand or agree on what the fluid released during squirting is. Some insist it's simply urine, others consider it female ejaculate, containing prostate hormones similar to those found in semen. Either way, it's a thing.

Orgasms from masturbation ruin your orgasms with a partner

Masturbation does not mess up your chances of orgasm during partnered sex, but a 2016 study shows that it doesn't increase your chances of an orgasm with a partner either if you feel very body conscious, feel under pressure to orgasm or your relationship is unstable[38]. Masturbation and exploring your body are the best way to learn what works for you. You can share your self-knowledge with a partner, they then also have the information to help you to orgasm.

It's also great to have this knowledge about your partner; orgasm isn't the goal of sex and knowing both how to give and receive pleasure during sex with a particular partner makes everything far more enjoyable for everyone. The key here is to share the knowledge you have learned about yourself. The more orgasms you have, the better you understand the differing ways you can have them. This feeds back positively into your lifeforce, causing want and desire to have more of them.

Good sex is when you have an orgasm

Think back to the most erotic experience you have had. What made it so memorable? It may have involved an explosive orgasm, but it's

[38] Kontula, O., 2017. Determinants of Female Sexual Orgasms. *The Journal of Sexual Medicine*, 14(5), p.e219.

probably not the most crucial part of the memory. Foreplay, setting, your connection with your partner, the intensity of the experience all plays a role. Also it may have been the anticipation, eroticism or feeling free that made it memorable. Remember, women can orgasm alone 95% of the time, if our sexual pleasure is measured by the incidence of orgasm, we would never want to share it with another person.

Women don't get physically frustrated when they can't orgasm

The experience men can have known as "blue balls" (the feeling of frustration, anger and genital discomfort from unresolved sexual stimulation), has a female equivalent often called "pink walls". Women can experience pain across the whole vulva or a painfully throbbing clitoris, and the same feelings of frustration and anger. We can be just as sexually frustrated as men.

You should be having multiple orgasms when you have sex

Women can stay at a heightened level of arousal after orgasm and experience a second (or third or fourth) orgasm in rapid succession. According to research only about 15% of women have experienced multiple orgasms[39], meaning 85% don't, so if you are in that 85%, there is no reason that you should be having them.

Faking orgasms to make your partner feel good is part of a woman's sex life

In the long run it might feel like you are doing your partner a favour, but it doesn't help anyone. Faking orgasms is a form of lying both to your partner and yourself. If you fake orgasm, you neglect your own sexual satisfaction; it signals to your partner all is well and that what just occurred totally works for you. Our partners want to please us, our

---

[39] Kontula, O., 2017. Determinants of Female Sexual Orgasms. *The Journal of Sexual Medicine*, 14(5), p.e219.

orgasms are important to them, so if you are faking it you are reinforcing an action that doesn't do it for you and not exploring ways that might. We essentially dig ourselves into a big hole of dissatisfaction and our partner is none the wiser, thinking everything is orgasmic. Yes, it can be disappointing for a partner when we don't experience orgasm, but that can usually be resolved with open and honest communication.

I often have women tell me that their partners tell them "No one else has complained," or "It's always worked with previous partners,", I point out that perhaps the previous partner faked it. Also, how we get to the point of orgasm is individual; it's not a 'one way fits all' thing.

So why do women fake orgasm so often? Because women are taught to believe a partner's sexual confidence is more important than our own pleasure, and that the most common way to have a partnered orgasm is actually the way they are least likely to. Women also do this because they believe that they should have orgasmed, and they feel shame when they don't. The phrase *fake it until you make it* really doesn't end well in this situation; think of it as "believe it until you achieve it" and then explore with a mindset of curiosity.

So how do you know if you have had an orgasm?

This may sound like a ridiculous question, but I see many women that don't know if they have orgasms or not, think they haven't but upon further questioning probably have, but it wasn't the earth moving experience they were expecting. I also see women who are sure they have not orgasmed but are told by their partners that they do, because the partner somehow knows their body better than them.

Medically speaking, an orgasm can be defined as the changes in the body when there is intense pleasure, causing an increase in pulse rate and blood pressure. Orgasms can also cause spasms of the pelvic muscles that cause contractions in the vagina. Neurochemicals are released during orgasm; an orgasm can feel like a sensual trance and create a state of sexual ecstasy that you can feel both physically and psychologically. An orgasm is heightened sexual excitement and gratification, followed by relaxation.

Physical signals

o Heart beats faster
o Breathing quickens becoming heavy
o Nipples become erect (not always apparent if you have inverted nipples)
o Genitals become engorged with blood and can feel fuller or swollen
o Contractions in your vagina
o Pelvic lifting or thrusting
o Curling of the toes or fingers
o Moaning (although many people don't)
o A deep sense of release through the body
o A sense of euphoria

While the physical process is similar for everyone, the actual orgasmic feeling varies from woman to woman and experience to experience. You might feel a mild tingle one time (how most women describe a "weak" orgasm) or an explosive full-body euphoria the next. If you're not sure whether you've reached orgasm, you probably haven't; the feeling is distinct, even if it's just a tingle.

What can make having an orgasm difficult and how do you overcome those difficulties?

There are many things that can make reaching and embracing orgasmic pleasure problematic. Most of those issues fall into three broad categories; many women can fall into more than one category and the categories themselves can overlap.

o Medical and physical
o Psychological and emotional
o Skills and communication (Chapters 11,12 and 13).

There are many medical and physical reasons that can cause problems with reaching orgasm. The most common ones are:

o Diabetes
o Hypertension
o Crohn's disease
o Vascular disease
o Chronic pain
o Autoimmune diseases
o IBS (Irritable Bowel Syndrome)
o Chronic constipation
o Fibromyalgia
o Chronic fatigue syndrome
o Hormone imbalance
o Oestrogen insufficiency caused by menopause (menopause is not a medical condition)
o Alcoholism
o Drug abuse or misuse
o Effects caused by smoking
o Anxiety and Depression
o Pelvic surgery or injury

Some medications can also impact on orgasm:

o SSRI antidepressants
o Anti-anxiety medications
o Blood pressure medications
o Hormonal supplements
o Antipsychotics

There are many things your doctor can do to support you, from referring you to a specialist to altering medication. To do that, they need to know what you are experiencing and how that is impacting you. Many women can find it difficult or embarrassing to talk about problems with orgasm or sexual function in general and suffer in silence. Doctors are used to talking about sexual function and most understand how important it is to a person, to their relationships and to general wellbeing. So have that chat with your doctor, they will support you.

Physical inactivity (or over activity) can also impact on your orgasmic capacity. But we are not talking about taking up marathon running here - your physical health is part of your lifeforce and it's important where possible to move your body. Your body is also part of your sensuality and how you experience the world. How you feel about your body is also an essential factor. Activities like gentle yoga and pelvic floor exercises to either improve tone or relax muscles and ligaments are very effective in improving not only orgasmic capacity, but also lubrication, comfort, arousal and desire. A 2010 study of 40 women found that after the completion of yoga sessions[40], the sexual function was significantly improved. The improvement occurred as increased desire, arousal, lubrication, orgasm, satisfaction, and a decrease in pain. The improvements were more prominent in women aged 45 and above.

---

[40] Dhikav, V., Karmarkar, G., Gupta, R., Verma, M., Gupta, R., Gupta, S. and Anand, K., 2010. Yoga in Female Sexual Functions. *The Journal of Sexual Medicine*, 7(2), pp.964-970.

Pelvic floor yoga poses

Embrace Technique

Resources available at www.KazRileyWoman.com

21.   *Sensation and pleasure pulse*

This involves contracting, relaxing and pulsing the muscles of your pelvic floor, which holds your uterus and bladder in place. The aim is to improve the tone of these muscles or relax them. This can help to improve some forms of urinary incontinence, increase strength and awareness of the muscles involved in pleasurable sexual sensations, reduce vaginal or pelvic pain during sex, all of which can help some women achieve orgasm. By identifying these muscles and being able to pulse them in a sensual rhythmic movement, you can connect to these muscles in a positive way. Many women report that they become more orgasmic, or their orgasms become stronger after doing this for a period of a few weeks.

- First of all, you need to identify the right muscles to contract, relax and pulse.

- Stop the stream of your urine while you're urinating; by contracting your pelvic floor muscles, they will feel like they are lifting.

- Once you have identified the muscles, you can practice and experiment anywhere, you don't need to be urinating.

- At first, aim to hold your contractions for 2 to 3 seconds and then release.

- Now pulse the muscles gently rather than squeeze them tight - this is a rhythmic sensual movement.

- Experiment with the strength of contraction and the speed, do this mindfully, notice how it feels.

- Be curious about the sensations it causes and what feels good to you.

- Practice doing this when you are fantasising and/or masturbating, breathing comfortably as you do.

Psychological and emotional

As with all of our sexual pleasure, there is a substantial psychological and emotional aspect to our orgasms. To allow ourselves to let go and feel bewitched with pleasure requires us to fully embrace the erotic journey and the experiences that take us to that point. We need to have knowledge about our bodies, feel comfortable within them and feel strong in our lifeforce. The psychological blocks to orgasm are the same as the ones that muddy the waters of our erotic bathtubs and supress desire, eroticism, arousal and sensuality: guilt, shame, the fear of negative judgement, negative body image, etc.

So why do so many women have a more difficult time orgasming with a partner even when they can orgasm through masturbation?

Our ability to orgasm through masturbation in private compared to our ability to orgasm with a partner are very different things. Most studies show that the ability to orgasm through masturbation is not a good indicator of being able to orgasm in the presence of a partner[41]. It's really about how comfortable we are with ourselves, sexuality, expressing sexual pleasure and our body image in the presence of someone else, or what we feel is expected from us. It does, however, stand to reason that if you are able to bring yourself to orgasm, then in the right "situation" with a partner, where you feel safe, unjudged, not under pressure and comfortable in your arousal, it will be much more likely to happen.

On the flip side, my clients and research reports that when women experience problems with orgasm with a partner they start to get anxious about being able to orgasm when masturbating alone, so orgasm through masturbation eventually becomes more difficult as well[42]. They see the orgasm as the problem rather than: (1) the situation they are in; or (2) how they feel when in different situations.

The term *situational anorgasmia* means that in some situations a woman can orgasm and in some she cannot.

For the purpose of this book, we will look at the three most common situations a woman tries to orgasm:

o Through penetration with a partner.
o In the presence of a partner through various means.
o Masturbating alone (Chapter 11).

[41] Kontula, O., 2017. Determinants of Female Sexual Orgasms. *The Journal of Sexual Medicine*, 14(5), p.e219.

[42] McCabe, M., 2009. Anorgasmia in Women. *Journal of Family Psychotherapy*, 20(2-3), pp.177-197.

As we have discussed, many women believe that they should be able to orgasm through penetration alone; they are unaware that 80% of women have never been able to do this. My work has shown me that figure can be improved considerably, but is dependent on a number of factors:

o Their clitoris happens to be relatively low and a short distance from the vaginal opening.
o The clitoris is relatively prominent externally.
o They are well lubricated naturally.
o They are in the correct position for the internal parts of the clitoris to be stimulated.
o They are so aroused they are yearning for penetration.
o There is rhythm and pattern to sexual movement.
o They can orgasm in the presence of a partner by other ways than penetration.
o They are pleasure focused rather than orgasm focused.
o They don't feel time pressured.

I would argue that if orgasm through penetration alone is dependent on those factors, then it isn't actually orgasm through penetration alone. It is better framed as an orgasm that occurs whilst being penetrated and a lot has happened prior to the penetration; it is most certainly not a singular event. I passionately believe that the difficulty to orgasm through penetration alone is not a dysfunction, it is entirely normal and as soon as the general population accepts that, the incidence of anxiety based sexual dysfunction for both men and women will decrease.

Research tells us that outside of a physical or medical issue preventing orgasm, the keys to more frequent orgasms for women lay in mental and relationship factors[43]. These factors and capacities include:

o Less focus on orgasm importance.

[43] Kontula, O., 2017. Determinants of Female Sexual Orgasms. *The Journal of Sexual Medicine*, 14(5), p.e219.

o Sexual desire.

o Sexual self-esteem and confidence.

o Openness of sexual communication with partners.

o Ability to concentrate on one's own pleasure.

o Mutual sexual initiations.

o A partner's good sexual techniques.

o A relationship that felt good and worked well emotionally.

o Sex was approached openly and appreciatively.

o Received more oral sex.

o Had longer-lasting sexual intimacy (not penetration).

o Asked for what they wanted in bed.

o Engaged in sexual emails or calls with a partner.

o Expressed love during sex.

o Acted out or had sexual fantasies.

o Embraced novelty.

Looking at this list, it starts to become apparent why some women can orgasm during an experience with a partner that may or may not involve penetration and why some can find that difficult. When we consider the importance of eroticism, safety, mystery and novelty to feed our desire, that anticipation is a vital part of us wanting to have sex, connection and intimacy. That we have clear boundaries and view ourselves in a positive light. We can then engage better with a partner, share and feel our way through a sexual experience rather than thinking and judging our way through it.

All of the Embrace Techniques outlined so far throughout this book have helped you to:

o Connect with yourself.

o Have better communication sensually and sexually.

o Enhance your sensuality.

o Listen to yourself and your body.

o Let go of shame, guilt and fear.

o Have healthy boundaries that you feel secure and safe within.
o Embrace fantasy, eroticism and desire.
o Understand your sexual function.
o Luxuriate in your arousal.

All are vital for sexual pleasure and orgasm.

If we are monitoring and judging, constantly thinking about what comes next, performing our arousal and pleasure, are anxious about what we look like, wondering if we are good lovers and thinking that we won't orgasm…it makes sense that we are less likely to orgasm when with another person. If we compare that to a person masturbating when alone, many of the factors that determine orgasm success with a partner are not applicable. When a person masturbates, their focus is inward, they just allow the feelings and sensations to flow, they may have erotic images and fantasies drifting through their minds. They are not wondering if they are making the right noise, if their belly is too flabby, if they are being a good lover. It's just them, their feelings, sensations and thoughts. There is no performance - just pleasure.

We don't think about how we express our arousal; we are not on show or wondering what the other person might be thinking about our skills, body or the time we are taking. We usually feel safe and relaxed. We are usually just feeling and accepting the sensations we experience and the pressure to orgasm is less than in a partnered situation. Generally, women that can orgasm with a partner can orgasm alone, so although being able to orgasm alone doesn't increase your chances of orgasming with a partner, not being able to would most likely hinder it.

From a survey I carried out of 500 women, those that could orgasm with a partner had three things in common:

o They were comfortable with themselves.
o They allowed themselves to reach orgasm rather than force it.
o They masturbated in various ways and methods, meaning that they didn't rely on one approach to orgasm.

Stop trying so hard

But to orgasm in any situation, alone or in the presence of a partner, we need to do something that for many people can be very difficult. They need to want to orgasm, expect to orgasm but not try to *make* themselves orgasm.

¿"The more willing you are to surrender to the energy within you, the more power can flow through you."

- SHAKTI GAWAIN

The psychological principle, the law of reversed effort

The harder you try to do something, the more likely the opposite will happen.

Imagine a time you couldn't sleep. Perhaps you were exhausted and ready to fall into a deep slumber, your bedroom was comfortable, you had your favourite blanket, it was the usual time you would go to sleep, nothing terrible had happened that day. But for some reason, there you were: wide awake. Perhaps you started looking at the clock on the bedside table thinking to yourself, why is this taking so long? So you tried harder to go to sleep, willing yourself to go to sleep, almost trying to force yourself into a dreamy state, but no, still awake.

Now thoughts start running through your mind, why am I awake? What if I can't sleep? Will I keep my partner awake if I'm tossing and turning all night long? How will I function at work tomorrow? Will I sleep tomorrow night? Then you realise you are nearly asleep, so you jerk awake again with the realisation that you were almost asleep. Now you are more awake than ever. You start scanning your body for signs of sleep, becoming so anxious you give up and get out of bed. The harder you tried to sleep the more awake you become.

The law of reversed effort can play a significant role in anorgasmia. This is especially true for partnered sex but can also stop an orgasm in its tracks when masturbating. Women often try really hard to orgasm, so much so that they are thinking or worrying about it as soon as they start to become intimate sexually with someone, or even before. Everything becomes focused on this one orgasmic event, they are never luxuriating in their sexual arousal and letting it build. They are monitoring and judging their bodies, questioning if they are ready for the next stage, focusing on making the sensations stronger, wondering "will I cum this time?" They become anxious, their minds filling with questions and doubts, willing themselves towards climax. They have become orgasm chasers, in hot pursuit of the earth-shattering big O.

They are no longer on a sensuous and enchanting sexual journey, taking in the magnificent landscapes along the way, stopping off here and there, taking time to be immersed in wonder of the place they are in right now, not thinking about how long the journey takes, perhaps not even wanting it to end because it's so beautiful. They have become the anxious commuter on a delayed train and running late for a meeting, wondering if they should walk, take the bus or jump in a taxi to the office to make up the lost time, fearing whatever they do they may miss their scheduled meeting and how disappointing and frustrating that will be. They have forgotten to GLIDE, or maybe they didn't even realise they needed to.

GLIDE into Arousal

→ Give yourself permission to receive pleasure.
→ Luxuriate in your arousal.
→ Ignore time.
→ Desire to be penetrated is overwhelming.
→ Ease up and slow down.

Research also suggests that the law of reverse effort could be an important factor with orgasmic release. One of the findings from a 2016 study stated:

"Women increasingly view sexual interaction through a more analytical lens, rather than casting their body and soul into enjoying sexual experiences with a partner and realizing their own desires. Excessive rationalism is the biggest enemy of orgasms. Simply put, thinking does alight desire, but orgasms come when thinking ceases."[44]

Orgasm is attainable for the majority of women both alone and in the presence of a partner, it is also attainable for most women to orgasm during penetration, providing the desire to be penetrated was overwhelming prior to penetration occurring. To find our orgasmic bliss, we need to not focus on or be judgmental about our ability to orgasm. We also need to not judge our partner's ability to make us orgasm, but to see orgasm as more than a singular physical event, to embrace it as one possible part of a mind and body experience that includes sensuality, connection, communication, knowledge, arousal and eroticism. Orgasm relies upon our erotic bathtubs to be overflowing and our ability to luxuriate in our arousal. This way we are focused on what is happening now, on how good something feels, and not concerning ourselves with what happens next. We glide through an experience either alone or with a partner, gloriously transitioning from one part of the journey to the next, taking our time, unsure what the next part of the journey might bring. If we have difficulty orgasming in the presence of a partner, we need not to ask "What is wrong with me?" but rather "What is going on here in this situation and is everything I need taking place? Am I free of shame? Am I overwhelmed with desire and/or arousal? Am I trying too hard? "Do I feel pressured?" Am I more concerned about my partner's ego than my own pleasure? Am I the stressed-out commuter, or am I enjoying this journey?"

---

[44] Kontula, O., 2017. Determinants of Female Sexual Orgasms. *The Journal of Sexual Medicine*, 14(5), p.e219.

CHAPTER ELEVEN

Mindful masturbation
The big 'O'
(Part Two)

"Everyone does it, but no one talks about it," Gloria said. About the different levels of skill involved. You have to practice before you become a great masturbator."

- URSULA HEGI, *HOTEL OF THE SAINTS*

Most women can orgasm through masturbation. The many ways that women masturbate are as diverse as women are themselves. Some use dildos, vibrating rabbits and clitoral stimulators. Others rub up against or ride a pillow, and some find that jets of water from the shower flowing over their vulva or clitoris is the key to orgasmic pleasure. Many just use their fingers or squeeze their thighs together. For many women, how they discovered masturbation, or that they even could, was by accident. Many of my clients tell me that they found a technique that felt good and would use it to self-soothe when they were younger, even before they knew that their sensations were called arousal or orgasm.

During the consultation at my office, women are often even more embarrassed talking about masturbation than about sex, constantly looking downward and shifting about uncomfortably in the chair. Female masturbation is still a taboo subject for many, or an activity that can be filled with shame, especially when a woman can masturbate alone and achieve orgasm but struggles to orgasm in the presence of a partner. But if you walk into any adult store, or browse online, or watch the commercials on TV that appear in the evenings, the majority of sex toys are aimed at women. In 2020, the sex toy industry was valued globally at 33.64 billion U.S. dollars and is projected to increase to 52.39 billion U.S. dollars by 2028. Over 60% of that figure was the female-centric market.[45]

The range of sex and self-pleasure toys available to us is massively more varied and has become ever more focused on the sensations that work for us. So we can ditch the taboo, because from the toy sales alone we know most women are masturbating, and there are many great reasons we might want to. Masturbation and sex both cause your body to release feel-good chemicals. Dopamine is one of the "happiness hormones" that is related to your brain's reward system. Endorphins are also released and are the body's natural pain reliever. Endorphins have de-stressing and mood-boosting effects. Oxytocin, often called the love hormone, is associated with feelings of bonding. Testosterone improves stamina, desire and arousal in both men and women, and is also released when you have sexual fantasies (so another great reason to indulge in your eroticism). Prolactin, the hormone that plays an essential role in lactation, influences your mood and immune system positively.

[45] Grand View Research, 2021. *Sex Toys Market Size, Share & Trends Report Sex Toys Market Size, Share & Trends Analysis Report By Type (Male, Female), By Distribution Channel (E-commerce, Specialty Stores, Mass Merchandizers), By Region,*. Grand View Research.

The other good news is that practice makes perfect; the more you masturbate, the more intense and satisfying your orgasms become[46] and as they become more frequent, it gets easier to reach orgasmic heights.

So does it matter how you masturbate?

The answer to this question is both yes and no. There is definitely no wrong way to masturbate, what you may want to consider is how many different ways you do it. It's a case of the more the merrier. If you use just one method of masturbation, then unless you have shared that information with a partner or it's completely different to how you might try and experience orgasm with a partner, when it comes to partnered sex, you may run into difficulty.[47]

Many women I work with say, "There is only one way I can get off (orgasm)," but the more ways you find to self-pleasure, the more orgasmic you will become. It makes sense that if you only masturbate by using a super powerful vibrator that forces an orgasm out of you, you may run into trouble if you try to achieve orgasm with your or a partner's fingers. Variety is definitely the spice of life here. If you are a woman that has never orgasmed, the chances are you just haven't found a way that works for you yet; maybe you have just been trying too hard or maybe you are just not sure how to masturbate. The website OMGYES.com is a fantastic resource as a "How to" guide for masturbation. Made for women and by women, based on research. OMGYES has many videos of women showing you how they masturbate; it is explicit, but tasteful and informative.

---

[46] Rowland, D., Donarski, A., Graves, V., Caldwell, C., Hevesi, B. and Hevesi, K., 2019. The Experience of Orgasmic Pleasure during Partnered and Masturbatory Sex in Women with and without Orgasmic Difficulty. *Journal of Sex & Marital Therapy*, 45(6), pp.550-561.

[47] Rowland, D., Hevesi, K., Conway, G. and Kolba, T., 2020. Relationship Between Masturbation and Partnered Sex in Women: Does the Former Facilitate, Inhibit, or Not Affect the Latter?. *The Journal of Sexual Medicine*, 17(1), pp.37-47.

I would highly recommend you check out this amazing resource; my clients find it to be more than worth the investment, which is less than many sex toys.

The many variations of masturbation

There are some common themes that are within the varied ways women masturbate. The more you involve all of your senses and eroticism in the build-up to orgasm, the more intense orgasms are. 77.2% of women report that more intense orgasms result from spending more time to build up arousal, bit by bit[48]. So give yourself time and permission to do this, with a mindset of playful curiosity. Be pleasure focused, rather than orgasm focused - use fantasy and find as many ways as possible to give yourself pleasure and to reach orgasmic bliss. Remember, your body is a vessel that you have been learning to fill with pleasure throughout this journey we are taking together. Masturbation is a great time to allow yourself to really experience all of your newfound sensuality. Your clitoris is the destination of your arousal, not the source, so draw your orgasm towards you, invite it into your body. Resist the temptation to force it.

Circles, spirals and ovals

Many women love the feeling of circles on or around their clitoris, or the whole vulva area. Some women love the anticipation of ever decreasing circles that start so vast they go from thigh to thigh and end up on or near the clitoris. Ovals are another favourite, either horizontally across the top of the clitoral hood or vertically around the clitoral region, including the parts of the clitoris that we can't see that are under the skin.

Teasing suggestion

Anticipation is your ally during both masturbation and partnered pleasure. Nearly (but not quite) touching a sensitive part of the vulva or clitoris

---

[48] Herbenick, D., Fu, T., Arter, J., Sanders, S. and Dodge, B., 2017. Women's Experiences With Genital Touching, Sexual Pleasure, and Orgasm: Results From a U.S. Probability Sample of Women Ages 18 to 94. *Journal of Sex & Marital Therapy*, 44(2), pp.201-212.

makes it so much sweeter and more effective than simply just touching from the get-go. Resist the urge to touch a particular spot until the desire is overwhelming; it will help your whole-body fill with pleasure rather than trying to spread it out to the rest of your body from your clitoris.

Repetition and consistency

With whatever motion you're doing in that moment, repetition and consistency make the feeling grow into full orgasm for a significant number of women. The approach to orgasm is a distinct phase in arousal, when even small changes have significant impact. It's also worth pointing out that in partnered sex, when a partner senses a woman is close to orgasm, they can often increase the speed, or pressure of touch or penetration which actually makes it harder for the woman to orgasm. So remember, not harder, not softer, not faster, not slower, not a different movement - precisely the same. This also doesn't mean the same way for each time you masturbate, just for this time.

Variation

Consistency during a single session of masturbation can help, but mixing up the ways you masturbate can really help you find new orgasmic height. During different sessions, experiment with:

* Different positions - standing, sitting, laid down, legs open or closed.
* Methods - fingers, dildos, glass wands vibrating eggs, internal vibrators, clitoral vibrators, sucking simulators, running water.
* Temperatures - cool, warm and hot (just make sure not too extreme to cause harm).
* Speed - experiment with different speeds of touch with your fingers or the speed settings on your toy.
* Pressure - notice what kinds of pressure work for you and notice whether that changes the more aroused you become. Sometimes less is more.

Rhythm

Experiment with different rhythms; you can skip beats, keep it constant or make up your own tune. Many toys have different rhythm settings, so find a groove that works for you.

Emphasis

You might find that emphasising certain parts of a motion works well, some women find that a circular motion where half the circle is quick, and the other half slow is tantalising, or every third movement is slower than the rest, for example.

Edging

This is where you bring yourself close to orgasm but stop just short, then build up all over again, over and over. Many women that struggle to orgasm find this very useful, as it switches the focus from trying to orgasm to trying not to, this is where the law of reversed effort can help you; it also makes you focus on the sensations keeping you in your body and out of a judging state in your head.

Breathing

Experiment with your breathing - many women naturally hold their breath when they are nearing orgasm. Be curious what happens if you make yourself breathe slowly and rhythmically, or if you breathe in and out quickly. You can also do this when you're not masturbating and notice the changes in your breath. Be mindful when doing this if you are asthmatic. You know your body; do what feels good to you.

Embrace Technique

Resources available at www.KazRileyWoman.com

22.   *Orgasmic breathing*

- Breathe in and out through your mouth, rhythmically and quickening in speed overtime. Do this several times and stop if you feel lightheaded.

- Now with each breath, tilt your pelvis back and forth.

- Now add in an up and down movement from your diaphragm. Notice the sensations....do this several times (stop if you get too lightheaded).

- Now add in a tilt from your upper chest and neck in time with your breath. Notice the sensations, do this several times (stop if you get too lightheaded).

- Now arch your head with your breath. Hold your breath for fifteen seconds and clench your body.

- Exhale and notice what happens, you may need to do this a few times before anything does, or add it into your masturbation practice.

Orgasmic pleasure trances

When describing sex and sexual pleasure, people talk of being entirely consumed by pleasure and the sensations it brings, that everything in the background disappears for a while, you can forget where you are, you are just in that very moment. As if you are in a trance.

Well, you *actually* are in a trance, and there is research to prove it. In a 2016 neuroscience study regarding what orgasms actually are[49], the researcher Adam Safron, found that "sex is a source of pleasurable sensations and emotional connection, but beyond that, it's actually an altered state of consciousness." The study reported that rhythmic stimulation to the brain can enhance neural oscillations at corresponding frequencies, a bit like rhythmically swinging back and forth on a swing. This process is called neural entrainment. It means if sexual stimulation is intense enough and goes on long enough, synchronised activity could spread throughout the brain. Your mind body connection is powerful. The study also found that: "This synchrony may produce such intensely focused attention that sexual activity outcompetes usual self-awareness for access to consciousness, so producing a state of sensory absorption and trance. This may be crucial for allowing for a sufficient intensity of experience to trigger the mechanisms of climax".

So, let yourself trance out - it doesn't mean that you are not paying attention, more that you are becoming enchanted by the process and are absorbed by it. One of the techniques I use with my clients to help then find neural entrainment is through a hypnotic technique called The Ember Within. I take them through a process that focuses them internally, imagining a sensual orange ember within them that begins to glow ever brighter and becomes more intense. It's quite a journey my clients experience, filled with euphoria, bliss and high levels of arousal all created within them, fully clothed and not being touched by anyone.

You can access an MP4 of The Ember Within at www.kazrileywoman.com **(Embrace Technique 23).**

Mutual masturbation

We tend to think of masturbation as typically a one-person activity. Mutual masturbation means two or more people are masturbating together or masturbating each other. This partnered play can happen in the same

---

[49] Safron, A., 2016. What is orgasm? A model of sexual trance and climax via rhythmic entrainment. *Socioaffective Neuroscience & Psychology*, 6(1), p.31763.

room or via video or phone. It is a great way to overcome sexual shyness or just enjoy hearing the sounds of a partner. When you masturbate with someone, you can watch, listen, help and encourage. You are part of each other's experience of pleasure, and this means you can see what your partner likes, and they can see what you like and how.

Mutual masturbation can make a massive difference to how you experience sexual pleasure because if you show someone how your body works, it puts them in a place of knowledge and stops them from having to guess when it comes to touching each other. Mutual masturbation is an incredibly intimate and erotic activity that helps break the pattern of orgasm focused sex. It is a fantastic way to learn about each other, create high arousal levels, and try out new things. Mutual masturbation is also a great way to introduce toys into a relationship. You get to show your partner just how brilliantly your sex toy works and how you like to use it. It can make you feel an exciting mix of vulnerable and powerful at the same time.

Another benefit of mutual masturbation is that it can help when having penetrative sex; most women need external clitoral stimulation to reach orgasm. If you are comfortable touching yourself with a partner, you can do this when you need a bit of extra stimulation without feeling shame or anxiety about what your partner is thinking. It means you stay in the moment and don't shift to judging - you are just feeling, enjoying and naturally embracing your sexual pleasure.

Practising penetration

Sexual pleasure with a partner is about good communication, how well you and your partner can articulate your needs and desires. Often, women just don't have the words to describe what they enjoy, or don't have enough experience to suggest other techniques. Recent research has looked at the sexual experiences of thousands of women and found out what made vaginal penetration more pleasurable for them[50]. They found a recurring pattern of four specific techniques that never had words to

---

[50] Hensel, D., von Hippel, C., Lapage, C. and Perkins, R., 2021. Women's techniques for making vaginal penetration more pleasurable: Results from a nationally representative study of adult women in the United States. *PLOS ONE*, 16(4), p.e0249242.

describe them before, and gave terms for each of these sexual methods to help women identify and communicate what feels best to them.

* **Angling.** Rotating, raising, or lowering pelvis and hips during penetration to adjust where inside the vagina, a toy or penis rubs.
* **Pairing.** A woman or her partner stimulates her clitoris with a finger or sex toy simultaneously with penetration.
* **Rocking.** The base of a penis or sex toy rubs against the clitoris constantly during penetration. Staying all the way inside the vagina, rather than thrusting in and out.
* **Shallowing.** Penetrative touch just inside the entrance of the vagina.

Having and using language for sexual techniques can be empowering. Women can feel comfortable and confident using them with partners and their partners also get a description of what the method is. To be able to describe what you like specifically, and to be able to ask for it, is incredibly beneficial for communication and also allows women to be flexible and explain what they want in the moment. Men really want to know what they can do to make you feel good. They enjoy it more if you enjoy it more. Having language that can quickly describe what you like is empowering to men, too.

Clitoral stimulation is vital; it isn't vaginal penetration that is most satisfying for the majority of women. Methods like shallowing and rocking really bring women extreme pleasure. This information is essential for men to know as well. Both men and women have been fed misinformation from society and from watching unrealistic porn, where women are usually deriving all their pleasure from penetration.

If you experiment with a sex toy during masturbation, you can understand how you like to be penetrated and how you don't, as well as how deeply and what kinds of speeds and movements. You can then share this knowledge with a partner.

CHAPTER TWELVE

Tantalising toys

Tools for masturbation, self-pleasure devices and sex toys come in a mind-boggling array of variations, styles and purposes. There is something for everyone and lots of tantalising sensations to choose from. Sex toys are a lot of fun, can help you understand your body better and be a part of your sensual journey to embracing your sexual pleasure and finding orgasmic bliss. When it comes to sex toys, variety is the spice of life and you might like to experiment with a wide range of types and sensations. They are also a lot of fun during partnered sex and can be used in many ways to enhance a sexual experience and create a lot of pleasure for everyone.

To get the best results from sex toys, remember to GLIDE - your clitoris is the destination of your arousal, not the source of it. Be pleasure focused rather than orgasm focused, and enjoy the process of mindful masturbation. Remember, the more ways you find to enjoy sexual pleasure, the more overflowing your erotic bathtub will become. Whatever sex toys you are using, your mind will *always* be your most powerful sex toy.

Original artwork by Melissa Zak
(Find her on Instagram @playboyknockoff)

TYPES OF SEX TOYS

Sex toys can be split into several broad categories. New ones are being developed all the time, many of which are much more focused on how women's bodies work and our pleasure.

Dildos are anything vaguely phallic (penis) shaped. They are used to simulate penile penetration. Some look like a realistic penis and come in various shapes, girths, lengths and colours. However, many are phallic-shaped but look nothing like a penis. Some have bumps and grooves, others are smooth and sleek. They can be straight, curved or very un-uniform. Dildos can be made of soft rubber, hard plastic, silicone, glass and metal. Traditionally, dildos have no vibrations, but many have an opening where a vibrator can be attached or inserted inside the dildo. Dildos are great for people who enjoy the feeling of being penetrated or like the feeling of fullness in their vagina or anus. If you are using a dildo for anal play, make sure the end of the dildo is flared and that part of the dildo (or anything you insert in your anus) always remains outside of the body. Glass and metal wands are a fantastic option for people who have discomfort or pain with penetration. They are frictionless, go in smoothly, are great for experimenting with temperature play because you can warm them up or cool them down. Glass and metal wands are also easy to clean.

Bigger isn't always better - think about any penetration experiences that have been pleasurable for you and what was too much or not enough. Then choose according to that information. Some women prefer a short and fat dildo, others long and slender, so go with what works for you. Insertable length is another consideration; you don't need to insert the entire dildo, go with your comfort level.

My clients' favourites in the dildo category are:

- ✓ Penis shaped dildos by New York Toy Collective[51].
- ✓ Smooth and curved dildos, such as the Ella Double-Sided Dildo by Lelo.
- ✓ Steel dildos, such as the Pure Wand Stainless Steel Dildo by nJoy.
- ✓ Glass Dildos, such as the Lovehoney Beaded Sensual Glass Dildo 7 Inch or the Lovehoney Tentacle Textured Sensual Glass Dildo.

Vibrators come in a massive range of shapes, sizes, intensities and varying purposes. Some have so many vibration patterns and settings, you would think they had been developed by NASA. Some are vibrating versions of dildos and others are not obviously sex toys to look at. When buying a vibrator, check:

- ✓ What speed and power settings they have. Is it intense enough or too much?
- ✓ How many different vibration patterns does it have? Varied settings can be helpful when helping your body to respond to many pleasure patterns.
- ✓ Is the vibrator rechargeable? Rechargeable toys are cheaper over time as you don't have to keep buying batteries.

---

[51] All product names and availability correct as of 2021.

✓ How loud is it? This can be a consideration if you are concerned about being overheard or you would find a noisy vibrator off-putting.

✓ What are the dimensions of the vibrator?

✓ Are you happy with the size?

✓ What is the vibrator made from and does that feel good to you?

✓ Is the vibrator waterproof? This is a consideration if you want to use it in the bath or shower.

Bullet vibrators are for clitoral stimulation and external clitoral contact. They are small, discrete and often inexpensive. They are mainly used on the clitoral glans but can be traced externally along the entire length of the vulva. My clients love the Bullet Vibrator from Wanderlust.

Clitoral vibrators are usually larger than bullet vibrators and typically more powerful. They can be shaped like eggs, tongues, be flat and wide to fit in the palm of your hand and can double up as an all-over body massager or an all-over vulva massager. My clients love the Sila from Lelo, Eva 2 from Dame and the Mimic Plus Rechargeable Waterproof External Vibrator from Clandestine Devices.

Rabbit vibrators have two essential parts. The main shaft of the toy is for internal use, and the rabbit ears stimulate your external clitoris simultaneously. My clients adore SORAYA WAVE™ from Lelo, Thrusting Rabbit Vibrator by GC and Fuzion Enigma 10 Speed by Rocks Off.

Wand vibrators are designed for external use. They're often quite large and sometimes mains powered. My clients love the Smart Wand 2 from Lelo and the Doxy Massager, The World's Most Powerful Wand Massager.

G-spot vibrators are designed for internal use and have a curved tip to stimulate your G-spot. My clients love the GIGI 2 Luxury Personal Massager G-spot Vibrator by Lelo.

Clitoral suction toys and massagers use air pressure or sonic waves to create gentle sucking sensations. They are a very different sensation from vibrators. If you love oral sex, these toys are magnificent. My clients rave about the SONA™ 2 Cruise from Lelo and the WOMANIZER Pro40 Red.

Butt plugs can feel good and can help create a feeling of fullness as the vaginal canal wall is next to the rectum. If you are wearing a butt plug and are then penetrated vaginally, this can help push the vaginal stimulation towards the internal clitoris. Butt plugs can be made of silicone, glass or steel. Remember, the rectum does not self-lubricate so you will need to add plenty of lube.

Cock rings were created initially to give men a more prolonged, fuller erection. Vibrating cock rings offer the same effect, while providing a buzzy sensation to the wearer and the partner being penetrated. This can help with clitoral stimulation during sex.

The sex toys myself and my clients love the most are the Lelo Enigma and the Lovehoney Beaded Sensual Glass Dildo. The Enigma is designed to stimulate the entire clitoris as well as the G-spot. Question marked in shape, one end pleasures the external clitoris with gentle sonic waves, while the other end is inserted into the vagina, where it vibrates in sync with the sonic waves to stimulate the internal clitoris and G-spot. The Enigma features eight different pleasure settings, is rechargeable, 100 percent waterproof, and quiet. The Enigma is my personal number one recommendation and the best female-centric sex toy ever invented; it's pricey but worth the investment. The Lovehoney Beaded Sensual Glass Dildo can be used in a variety of ways and is excellent for temperature play. The curves feel wonderful and it's easy to clean and hold.

The Lelo Enigma and Lovehoney Beaded sensual glass dildo
Photograph by John Steel Photography

CHAPTER THIRTEEN

Redefining great sex

"When sex becomes a production or performance, that is when it loses its value. Be mutual. Be loud. Be clumsy. Make noises, be quiet, and make a mess. Bite, scratch, push, pull, hold, thrust. Remove pressure from the moment. Love the moment. Embrace it. Enjoy your body; enjoy your partner's body. Produce sweat, be natural, entice your senses, give into pleasure. Bump heads, miss when you kiss, laugh when it happens. Speak words, speak with your body, speak to their soul. Touch their skin, kiss their goosebumps and play with their hair. Scream, beg, whimper, sigh, let your toes curl, lose yourself. Chase your breath; keep the lights on, watch their eyes when they explode. Forget worrying about extra skin, sizes of parts and things that are meaningless. Save the expectations, take each second as it comes. Smear your make-up, mess up your hair, rid your masculinity, and lose your ego. Detonate together, collapse together, and melt into each other."

- CORISSA MARIE

For women to find, understand and embrace our sexual pleasure, we need to change the way we traditionally think about what good sex is. Our focus must shift from the goal of orgasm to one of shared pleasure. If both women and men were to step off the late commuter train, trying to get from zero to the big O and step onto the magical mystery tour bus of sensuality and eroticism, everyone will have more satisfying and connecting experiences that bolster their lifeforce, both between the sheets and out of them. We can leave the notion behind that sex and sexual pleasure is a performance to be judged and that it follows a set pattern or formula, especially when that formula doesn't work that well for anyone. In a recent survey of 3,836 people[52], where both men and women were asked these two questions:

- The last time you had sex (intercourse, NOT foreplay), how long did it last?

- How long would you like sex (intercourse, NOT foreplay) to last?

The average answer from women for "How long would you like sex to last?" was 25 minutes 51 seconds. The men gave an average response of 25 minutes 43 seconds. So, expectations were similar for men and women. But across the board, when asked how long intercourse lasted the last time they had sex, the average was 15 minutes.

This 15-minute figure is much higher than the findings of past research, where intercourse lasted an average of 5.4 minutes[53]. Regardless, if intercourse lasts for 5 or 15 minutes, that is much shorter than the 25 minutes seen as the ideal. It can be deduced that both men and women expect that intercourse should last somewhere between forty to eighty per cent longer than it actually does for most people, and not only are they focusing on penetration and orgasm as the goal, when they get there, they believe that it didn't last long enough. This often translates to men

---

[52] saucydates.com. 2021. *How long does sex last?*. [online] Available at: <https://saucydates.com/how-long-does-sex-last/>

[53] Waldinger, M., Quinn, P., Dilleen, M., Mundayat, R., Schweitzer, D. and Boolell, M., 2005. ORIGINAL RESEARCH—EJACULATION DISORDERS: A Multinational Population Survey of Intravaginal Ejaculation Latency Time. *The Journal of Sexual Medicine*, 2(4), pp.492-497.

feeling like they orgasm too quickly and women feeling like they didn't orgasm soon enough, leaving everyone feeling like they are failing or not performing as they should.

These beliefs can lead to anxiety about sex; for men, they can become so anxious that they can have trouble getting or maintaining an erection or having the law of reversed effort kicking in, where they are so focused on not reaching orgasm that it becomes almost impossible not to (that is, it becomes almost inevitable that quick orgasm will occur.) Women, on the other hand, tend to become so focused on trying to orgasm that they cannot; this can also happen to men. In these situations, it is hardly surprising that sex can become more and more stressful and frustrating. People will often blame themselves for not satisfying their partner; feeling shame about their sexual performance; or blaming a partner for "not doing it right." This can cause so much stress that eroticism and sensuality become left out of the equation, desire and arousal become harder to access and sex becomes something to be avoided or endured. Simply put, they are focusing on the wrong thing.

Foreplay is really core-play

When we are taught about sex or it is shown to us in films, we are repeatedly shown that foreplay starts with a kiss or a look and everything after that is about reaching the goal, the main event: penetration and orgasm. But foreplay isn't about getting from zero to the big O, it's about sharing an enchanting experience with another person. It's about allowing ourselves to become so overwhelmed and focused on the shared pleasure that we surrender not to another person, but to our feelings, sensations and arousal. It is a process of never-ending curiosity and intrigue, fuelled by our eroticism, which then in turn fuels our passion and desire. It's all the little things that accumulate as we move through life, things that can turn up our arousal and get our erotic and sensual juices flowing. That process starts long before we are with another person - that curiosity and intrigue is very much part of our lifeforce.

As we have discussed throughout this book, our sexual pleasure starts in our minds. This is also true of great sex. It doesn't start from a first touch, it's about the thought and anticipation of what pleasure may await us and the many ways that might manifest. We do this through our sensuality, fantasy and memories of our past experiences, where our arousal was high and our inhibitions were low. If you think back to a time when you were really turned on, most likely you felt safe, the communication was good, you didn't feel pressured and you felt good about yourself. If we think back to the start of a relationship, we are curious about the other person, it's full of possibility and mystery and it's exciting stuff. I see many women and couples looking to have better sex; they are stuck in a rut or their desire seems to have left them. They get to a point when they can take or leave sex or they just don't want it at all. But when I start asking questions and digging a little deeper, the answers are always similar. Lack of time, inability to orgasm, too tired, head full of worries, body insecurity, worried that they are not satisfying to a partner, putting a partner's pleasure before their own and worrying about the consequences of that filling them with anxiety.

This is not only a female issue; I see worry and performance anxiety just as often with my male clients as my female ones. Almost always, it's about seeing sex as a performance or a test of endurance or skill, rather than a magical experience of discovery to be relished and enjoyed. Redefining great sex helps everyone. When we talk about reclaiming our sexual pleasure, it's very easy to fall into the trap of seeing this as a fight or a battle against men.

Undoubtedly, much of the repression of female sexuality was by men, but those men are long gone. Our challenge is against the legacy of the shame and misinformation left behind by that era. There will always be people (of any gender) that will hold onto the beliefs of old, but most people when they have the correct information are able to see things in a new light and take action accordingly. I am often told by women that their partners don't do enough foreplay or that they fake orgasms to save a partner's ego - they will often blame their partner for that. When I question these women if they ask for what they want or need sexually, or show their partner how to touch them, most tell me they do not or they are too embarrassed or ashamed to do that. I point out that the shame they carry is stopping them from expressing their needs to their partner, it's not that their partner is refusing to meet their needs.

We must remember that the men in our lives are taught the same things that we are about our bodies and sexual pleasure (often even less), that their sources of information are the same as ours. In many cases, they will have had partners fake orgasms and perform their arousal and not been aware that was happening. As you find, understand and embrace your sexual pleasure you need to share that information with your partner or future partner. If we take responsibility for our own sexual pleasure and exchange information with our partners, you can then embrace your sexual pleasure together. Then the fun really starts! People have the highest sexual satisfaction with partnered sex by having J.U.I.C.Y. sex. Like all good things in life, great sex requires you and your partner to put in a little work, you need to keep your erotic bathtub full. If you just leave it all to chance and hope when the moment comes everything will just fall into place… it probably won't.

JUICY SEX

💜 Judgement Free
💜 Unpredictable
💜 Intimate and Informed
💜 Communication and Consent
💜 Yearning and Reminiscing

Judgement free sex means no one is performing and no one is judging their own or a partner's performance. No one is being compared to or expected to respond like past partners did and there is no obsessing about orgasm. Judgement free sex means being curious about and exploring with another person, it's about paying attention, reading the other person and then responding. Knowing where both yours and your partner's sexual arousal "starting point" is moves you toward fulfilling sex. Some people can get in the mood instantly. Others need a cue to get aroused. Understanding and accepting those differences will help you connect. People who feel desire and arousal immediately can often feel rejected or frustrated that they are usually the one initiating sex. People who need a cue often worry that they don't have spontaneous desire and feel bad that they don't think about initiating sex. Knowing which you and your partner are, helps you let go of the frustration or worry. Judgment free sex is flexible, people who stay curious and adaptable about sex, tend to feel better about themselves, which in turn paves the way for a more fulfilling sex life.

People who are sexually satisfied understand that sex is about more than just intercourse.

Allow yourself to see sex and intimacy as a general term that includes a wide range of things: a flirty text message, a sensual massage, mutual masturbation or anything you like. This stops people feeling pressured or performative and takes away the need to chase after orgasms at a set moment.

Sex has no normal. What you like, how often you want it, and how important it is to you is different for everyone. It's easier to have judgement free sex when pornography is limited, as porn sets unrealistic expectations of what real-life sex is. That can chip away at a person's self-esteem and hurt their sexual confidence. Use your enchanting mind castle (Embrace Technique 16) to widen your definition of sex and experience judgement-free sexual experiences; it makes it easier to translate into the bedroom.

Unpredictable sex that isn't stuck in a rut and doesn't always follow the same pattern feeds your eroticism and desire. Be curious, experiment and have fun. If you don't know what might happen next, it keeps things

196

exciting and takes away the anxiety of being ready to move to the next part of the "pattern". Allowing your sex to be free-flowing and just doing what feels good at that moment or switching to something else if it doesn't, will enable you to be in your body rather than monitoring in your head. Free-flowing sex also allows you to ask for things and to be asked, the phrase "It would really turn me on if…" followed by whatever it is you think might be exciting to say and to hear. This is also a great way to positively redirect a partner if what is happening right now isn't doing it for you.

Experiment with different types of touch, words, positions, techniques, toys, and times of day. Talk about them out of the bedroom too. The anticipation of playful and curious experimentation can be a massive trigger for desire and talking about how good something felt fills your erotic bathtub for the next time. Unpredictability allows you to seize the moment if one unexpectedly turns up, it's exhilarating and feeds your lifeforce.

Intimate and informed physical contact is powerful and builds connection, intimacy and trust. Couples that touch and hug just because it feels good have a much easier time connecting when things become sexual. Touch takes pressure off sexual goals, touching or being touched in a certain way just because it feels good at that moment, serves to increase arousal and desire. Embrace Techniques 4, 5, 6, 7, 8, 9, 12, 13, 14 and Chapters 10,11 and 12 can help you here. There are many kinds of intimacy, but all of them involve focusing on each other and on an awareness of our own pleasure. Knowledge can equal sexual bliss. Learning more about your own body and each other's physical and mental erotic and erogenous zones; how much stimulation you need and how; and on what turns you on, can take your sex life to new heights. Couples that are willing to learn new things and share that knowledge or learn something together, experience improved intimacy. Take an online or in person erotic massage class, research things that intrigue you, give your partner this book to read. All of these things help you to broaden your sexual horizons and keep intimacy.

Consent and communication. Couples who are open and honest with each other about what they do and don't enjoy sexually and confide in each other - both in and out of the bedroom - are more likely to feel satisfied.

Share if your lifeforce is lacklustre, or if you have trouble reaching orgasm, if you feel self-conscious about your body or if anything is uncomfortable. Talk about your fantasies and dreams, exchange yes, no, maybe lists (Embrace Technique 15). Tell your partner what you want, hear your partner's needs, and then talk about them. Many people fall into the trap of just expressing what they don't want and not communicating what they *do* - the assumption being, if something is not on their "don't want" list means it's OK or they do want it, but a partner without the knowledge of what someone wants, is very much adrift with nothing much to guide them. Tell and ask, rather than leaving it to luck and guess work. Couples that communicate their desire, even when they know nothing can happen right now, also have better sex. Send the text from work that tells your partner you just had a wild and sexy thought about them, how they made you feel last night or something they did that was super sexy. Smile inside when you get a flirty communication from them. This kind of communication feeds the erotic aspect of your lifeforce and relationship; it's often something people stop doing after they marry or start cohabiting and then wonder why the desire disappears from their relationship.

Yearning and Reminiscing involves making time to make love and/or masturbate and is essential to your lifeforce and desire. If you allow sex to become such a low priority that it never happens this can also impact your desire and responsiveness. Simply you stop yearning and can often start resenting. Yearning comes from sex that feeds all of your senses and makes you feel amazing, we don't yearn for things that cause us to be anxious, cause us to feel shame or are physically painful. Great sex leaves us yearning for the next time. Reminiscing about the incredible experiences you have shared with a partner, especially when you don't have time for physical sex or are apart, is a great way to stay connected and keep the embers of desire burning. "Do you remember the time when we…" is a fantastic way to keep your erotic juices flowing, can cause arousal and keeps your erotic bathtub full. Juicy sex encompasses all the criteria expressed by women who had satisfying sex[54], such as:

[54] Kontula, O., 2017. Determinants of Female Sexual Orgasms. *The Journal of Sexual Medicine*, 14(5), p.e219.

- ✓ Less focus on orgasm importance.
- ✓ Sexual desire.
- ✓ Sexual self-esteem and confidence.
- ✓ Openness of sexual communication with partners.
- ✓ Ability to concentrate on one's own pleasure.
- ✓ Mutual sexual initiations.
- ✓ A relationship that felt good and worked well   emotionally.
- ✓ Sex was approached openly and appreciatively.
- ✓ Received more oral sex.
- ✓ Had longer-lasting sexual intimacy (not penetration).
- ✓ Asked for what they wanted in bed.
- ✓ Engaged in sexual emails or calls with a partner.
- ✓ Expressed love during sex.
- ✓ Acted out or had sexual fantasies.
- ✓ Embraced novelty.

It makes sense to focus on juicy sex rather than orgasm. Orgasm is more likely to happen *because* sex is juicy.

Embrace Technique

Resources available at www.KazRileyWoman.com

23.   *Look into my eyes...*

This Embrace Technique helps you to share your wants and needs and hear your partner's. It enables you to express gratitude for the things you may not acknowledge every day, or perhaps take for granted. People can feel a little silly at first when they do this, but with a bit of perseverance and lack of judgement, it's a potent and connecting process. In my therapy room, I take couples through a very similar process called mutual hypnosis. You can watch a video of that process on my YouTube channel, *Trancing in the Sheets*. You can also access an MP4 at www.kazrileywoman.com to guide you through the process of this Embrace Technique.

* Sit or lay opposite your partner so that you are facing each other, connect hands and gently gaze into each other's eyes. This is a gaze not a stare so blink as you need to. Doing this can feel a little strange at first, so don't worry if you laugh.
* Breathe slowly and deeply in through your nose and out through your nose. Allow yourselves to relax, keep gazing. Take your time with each of the following.
* Think about how much you love the person you are gazing at.
* Think about the things they do that make you happy (this could be anything from a hug to something they say).
* Think about the things they do that make you feel loved and protected.
* Think about the time you first met.
* Think about a time they held you close.
* Think about something you do or did together that connects you.
* Think about a sensual experience you have shared.
* Think about something they do that turns you on.
* Think about a time you were really turned on with your partner.
* Think about an erotic experience you have shared.
* Think about a sexual experience you have shared.
* Now take turns telling each other the following statements below. No judgement, just allow yourself to give the gift of telling and receive the gift of hearing.
* Tell your partner about how much you love them. Then, listen.
* Tell your partner about the things they do that make you happy (this could be anything from a hug to something they say) then listen.
* Tell your partner about the things they do that make you feel loved and protected, then listen.

* Tell your partner about the time you first met, then listen.
* Tell your partner about time they held you close, then listen.
* Tell your partner about something you do or did together that connects you, then listen.
* Tell your partner about a sensual experience you have shared, then listen.
* Tell your partner about something they do that turns you on, then listen.
* Tell your partner about a time you were really turned on with your partner, then listen.
* Tell your partner about an erotic experience you shared, then listen.
* Tell your partner about a sexual experience you have shared, then listen.
* Notice how you feel, notice what you want right now, share that too.

The tongue is mightier than the sword

For many women, one of the most extraordinary sexual experiences is oral sex. There is not only an oral sex (cunnilingus) gap when it comes to heterosexual partners - men tend to receive more than they give - but there's an enjoyment gap too[55]. Oral sex is the most common way for women to successfully reach orgasm with a partner. Having a partner's complete concentration on your clitoris, vulva, and vagina allows you to lie back and enjoy the pleasure to the fullest, if you give yourself permission to do that.

There is a lot of misinformation in our society that basically tells us that vulvas are dirty. Most women go through life feeling self-conscious about how they smell, look, taste, or all of the above. That feeling of

---

[55] Wood, J., McKay, A., Komarnicky, T. and Milhausen, R., 2016. Was it good for you too?: An analysis of gender differences in oral sex practices and pleasure ratings among heterosexual Canadian university students. *The Canadian Journal of Human Sexuality*, 25(1), pp.21-29.

vulva self-consciousness can make it hard to relax or stop you asking for or permitting oral sex. As long as you take care of your vulva, it is not dirty - it actually self-cleans. The problems usually start when we use highly scented soaps and other things on or in our vulvas to make us smell good; we knock out of whack a well-balanced system that keeps our vulvas clean. Our vulvas are not supposed to smell like roses or taste like we are dripping with sugar. Our vulvas are supposed to taste like vulvas, and because of the pheromones we produce, the smell and taste of a well-loved and nurtured vulva is usually a wonderful and welcome taste and scent to a partner. Women can feel vulnerable when receiving cunnilingus; being laid flat on your back with your legs spread apart is exposure in its fullest form. It also contradicts the concept of "good" girls keep their legs closed and you should be ashamed if you don't (Chapter 8 can help you let go of sexual shame). Because vulnerability is such a key factor when it comes to cunnilingus, covering up may help you into feel more comfortable. Receiving oral sex with your knickers still on, causing your partner to pull them aside can be incredibly sexy. You get to be partially covered, while your partner gets to reveal a prize underneath.

One of the most incredible resources about oral sex and probably one of the best "How to" guides ever written is Ian Kerner's book, *She Comes First: The Thinking Man's Guide to Pleasuring a Woman*. It is also great reading for women to better understand how to guide a partner during oral sex and that the wild lapping of vulvas we see in porn is really not going to have much effect. Buy the book; it's essential reading.

According to Kerner, my clients and personal experience, there are vital things that need to happen to make oral sex unforgettable.

* Foreplay is essential, and if you are yearning to be touched on your vulva well before that first oral kiss, you avoid trying to *become* aroused because you already *are* aroused. The clitoris isn't the source of your arousal even when it comes to oral sex.

* You need to be comfortable - getting cramp isn't sexy. Many women like being on their backs. Being above your partner on your knees, essentially offering your vulva (aka face sitting, a very misleading term) allows you to feel in control and move as you need to. Being stood up with your partner knelt before you is also very effective, but make sure you have something to lean back on, like a wall.
* Accept these three things. (1). There is no rush. (2). Your natural scent and taste is provocative and intoxicating. (3). The person going down on you is probably enjoying it as much as you are - most men find it a real turn on.
* Remember this is something you do with someone, not something being done to you. Move as you need to, ask for what you want, go with the flow.
* Give yourself permission to receive pleasure (Chapter 14).

Great sex can be defined in many ways and flavours, it is really anything that doesn't have the sole focus of penetration, so have fun with it and make it JUICY.

CHAPTER FOURTEEN

Permission for pleasure: the art of being able to receive

"Your body can be one of the greatest sources of pleasure when you open your five senses fully and experience the physical wonder of being alive. Pleasure can come in the form of sight, like when you see a magnificent sunset, or taste, like when you eat a favourite food. It can come as a glorious musical sound or the soft touch of a lover. The only secret to learning the lesson of pleasure is to make time and space for it in your life."

- CHERIE CARTER-SCOTT, *IF LIFE IS A GAME*

The ability to experience the feeling of pleasure is a joyous gift, the Oxford dictionary defines the word pleasure as "a feeling of happy satisfaction or enjoyment," and as a verb, "to give sexual enjoyment or satisfaction to someone." Humans are innately wired to seek pleasure in the things that feel, sound, look, smell and taste good to us. So it makes sense that humans evolved to find something that is essential to keep the species going very pleasurable; mainly sex, eating food and drinking water. As we have discussed throughout this book, historically society has done much to dampen and control women's pleasure. We have been taught that our pleasure, especially our sexual pleasure, is dangerous, morally problematic, and could get out of control. That as women, we *should* control our sexual pleasure and our desire for it to be acceptable.

In today's world, we often hear about guilty pleasures, which sends us the message that if we experience pleasure, we should also feel guilt. Remember, guilt is the feeling that "I did something bad." Sometimes shame creeps in, too: "I am bad because I experienced pleasure." Problems can occur when we experience something called false pleasure. False pleasure is when you check out, you are not tuning in, not listening to your body, and not immersed in the experience you call pleasure. A false pleasure is one you use to numb yourself, reward yourself, or escape from something. A piece of cake you eat with your full attention, savouring every mouthful and using all of your senses is a true pleasure - you are immersed in the experience. A whole cake you mindlessly eat standing up, watching a TV programme you don't enjoy, distracting yourself from the cake that you are eating and feeling guilty about, and eating to distract yourself from your life, is a false pleasure, conversely.

Advertising tells us what counts as pleasure: eating certain foods, drinking alcohol, watching TV, shopping and expensive holidays. These messages are really telling us that indulgence equals pleasure, that pleasure is something that we consume. On the whole we are shown false pleasures and those false pleasures are often bad for us, especially when we consume them in excess. We are bombarded by so many false pleasures that the true ones can pass us by. We can become so focused on what we might buy on a shopping trip, we don't see the beautiful scenery we drive past on the way to the mall. True pleasure is everywhere in life, from a beautiful flower to spending time with someone you enjoy the company of.

We also experience pleasure when we do something for someone else or when we permit them to do something for us. Sexual pleasure is usually a true pleasure, especially when we allow ourselves to be immersed in the experience using all of our senses, either alone or with a partner. It allows us to experience the joy of our bodies and the pleasure of someone else's. Sexual pleasure is also good for you. The benefits for women include:

- ☺ Lower blood pressure
- ☺ Better immune system
- ☺ Better heart health, possibly including lower risk for heart disease
- ☺ Improved self-esteem
- ☺ Decreased depression and anxiety
- ☺ Increased libido
- ☺ Immediate, natural pain relief
- ☺ Better sleep
- ☺ Increased intimacy and closeness to a sexual partner
- ☺ Overall stress reduction, both physiologically and emotionally

So, go ahead and give yourself permission to have and receive sexual pleasure - you do not have to earn it and you can feel wonderful about having it. Your capacity to experience physical, mental, emotional and sexual pleasure is there to be enjoyed and is good for you; there's no moral worth in denying *true* pleasure to yourself.

Our journey together so far has taught you how to find and understand your sexual pleasure, how to experience pleasure mindfully, with every one of your senses. You now know that true pleasure is everywhere, from the feeling of the sun on your skin, moving your body and everything else that fills your erotic bathtub and gives energy to fill your lifeforce hot air balloon. That the guilt we can feel and the shame we can experience can take away much of the true pleasure we can experience from our eroticism, sensuality and sexual pleasure. You have discovered many methods within the Embrace Techniques within this book to access and increase your true sexual pleasure. You have discovered how to create your personal boundaries, so that you can bring your sexual pleasure inside those boundaries, on your terms and in accordance with your life, beliefs, religion and circumstances and feel safe doing so. Now it's time to make a conscious and important decision. You need to let go of the past and promise to wholeheartedly give yourself permission to embrace your sexual pleasure, own it completely, and become immersed in your true sexual pleasure - both when alone and when you are with a partner from now on. This isn't deciding if you deserve it or not; it is much more clear-cut than that, this is an enthusiastic and ecstatic YES to yourself.

- ☺ **YES**, I am built for sexual pleasure.
- ☺ **YES**, I am primed for sexual pleasure.
- ☺ **YES**, I am responsible for my sexual pleasure.
- ☺ **YES**, I can have sexual pleasure.
- ☺ **YES**, I can ask for my sexual pleasure.
- ☺ **YES**, I enjoy sexual pleasure.
- ☺ **YES**, my sexual pleasure is part of me.
- ☺ **YES**, my sexual pleasure is part of being a woman.

You can check that you have embodied these yes's to yourself by going back to Embrace Technique 12 (***Hearing and respecting your own yes's and no's***) and feeling your body's response to the above statements. If you don't feel the "yes" response, go back and review:

1. Embrace Technique 9: ***Embracing your body***.
2. The Embrace Techniques in Chapter 6: ***Creating and calibrating your boundaries.***
3. The Embrace Techniques in Chapter 8: ***It's a shame***.
4. Ask yourself if there is a disruption in my lifeforce, and identify what it is or might be.
5. Ask yourself, do I feel safe? If not, what is making me feel unsafe?

Now that you have given yourself permission to embrace your sexual pleasure, you also need to give yourself permission to receive it when you choose to, without judging your reactions or being performative about it. It doesn't matter if your body is different in your sixties than in your forties or twenties; it's irrelevant if your arousal happened faster last week; and it makes no difference if you are quiet or make lots of noise. All the things that were keeping you in your head in the past... you need to accept them. Bodies change, people make sounds, our reactions are unique to that moment and no two experiences are the same. If we accept our sexual pleasure and treat every experience as unique, we become immersed in *that* moment. We don't compare it to our past experiences, how we imagined it might be or we think it should be. We are not judging or trying, we are present in our bodies and in that unique experience.

When we embrace something, it means we accept it. When we embrace sexual pleasure with a partner - in all the forms that may take - we must be willing to receive pleasure and give pleasure. One of the greatest gifts we can give another person is to receive pleasure from them, and to do that wholeheartedly, we need to be in a place where we accept not only the pleasure they give us, but also ourselves. To become immersed in the experience, we must stop wondering if what we are doing is good enough, or even if we are good enough. Then we become focused and feel good instead. We can feel good about feeling good, which makes our partners feel good too.

Embrace Technique

Resources available at www.KazRileyWoman.com

24. *Becoming immersed in pleasure*

This Embrace Technique is to help you become immersed in pleasure, it helps you to become ever more present in your body and to go with the flow of your pleasure and where that takes you.

☺ Take time to notice a feeling of comfort and calm in your body.

☺ Take time to notice noticing that feeling of comfort, notice as you do, it becomes more profound. A profound, pleasurable, comfortable feeling in your body.

☺ Notice the pleasurable feeling more, being more comfortable and being comfortable in pleasure.

☺ Give yourself permission to be deeper immersed in the feeling and feel more pleasure.

☺ It's easy, just tell yourself that you can now become immersed in a deeper level of pleasure, give yourself permission, go to that next level, that deeper level, giving yourself permission for more pleasure.

☺ Notice that it is far more intense, and more pleasurable, where do you feel it?

☺ Permit yourself to wonder what would happen if you were to give yourself permission to go into a deeper level of pleasure. How delicious and sublime that would feel…

☺ Give yourself permission to experience that and do that now… go deeper still and feel yourself become more immersed.

☺ Have these words in your mind: **I give myself permission to embrace pleasure.**

☺ Now slowly scan your body from the top of your head to the tips of your toes... notice any areas you don't feel pleasure in, and direct pleasure to these areas with your breath. Slow and deliberate breaths that breathe pleasure into those areas of your body. Give yourself permission to experience pleasure in those areas too.

☺ Just imagine what it would be like to go to the next level, where you can give yourself permission to experience pleasure in your life much more profoundly. Pleasure comes in so many forms: the sun, the feeling of rain, the sound of laughter, touch... You can feel those things, you can give yourself permission for pleasure in every area of your life.

☺ Now here is something really wonderful. Down at the next level is the permission to receive pleasure, not just to have pleasure, but to receive pleasure. To permit and allow someone else the pleasure of giving you pleasure, it would make another person so happy and that gives you even more pleasure. You can experience what an amazing gift it is to receive pleasure, to yourself and the person pleasuring you. This simple act of allowing yourself to receive pleasure, completely fully and whole heartedly. It is a wonderful gift to someone else.

☺ Really focus on that thought, how wonderful it is to receive pleasure now... Go to the next level, deeper, give yourself permission to receive pleasure, consciously, subconsciously, emotionally and physically.

☺ You can feel that wonderful sensation and knowledge of permitting yourself to receive pleasure...

☺ It's a pleasurable and sensual feeling to do this...perhaps tingling through your body in a pleasurable way.

☺ Every part of you can tingle and smile, with that absolute acceptance that you **can** experience pleasure, you can **accept** pleasure into your body and mind and you can **receive** pleasure from another person. It feels so good to do that. Feel good about feeling good.

☺ Keep going to deeper and deeper levels of pleasure; sensual pleasure, erotic pleasure, sexual pleasure... The deeper you go into this immersion of pleasure, the more pleasure you feel. Become completely immersed in pleasure and allow yourself to fully embrace it.

☺ Bring this pleasure inside your boundary, it is yours, you created it, you permitted it, you control it and who you share it with.

Embrace absolute acceptance of pleasure and your innate ability to experience it...

CHAPTER FIFTEEN

Awakening Aphrodite

"Imagine a woman who believes it is right and good she is a woman.

A woman who honours her experience and tells her stories.

Who refuses to carry the sins of others within her body and life.

Imagine a woman who trusts and respects herself.

A woman who listens to her needs and desires.

Who meets them with tenderness and grace.

Imagine a woman who acknowledges the past's influence on the present.

A woman who has walked through her past.

Who has healed into the present.

Imagine a woman who authors her own life.

A woman who exerts, initiates, and moves on her own behalf.

Who refuses to surrender except to her truest self and wisest voice.

Imagine a woman who names her own gods.

A woman who imagines the divine in her image and likeness.

Who designs a personal spirituality to inform her daily life.

Imagine a woman in love with her own body.

A woman who believes her body is enough, just as it is.

Who celebrates its rhythms and cycles as an exquisite resource.

Imagine a woman who honours the body of the Goddess in her changing body.

A woman who celebrates the accumulation of her years and her wisdom.

Who refuses to use her life energy disguising the changes in her body and life.

Imagine a woman who values the women in her life.

A woman who sits in circles of women.

Who is reminded of the truth about herself when she forgets.

Imagine yourself as this woman."

- Patricia Lynn Reilly, *Imagine a Woman*

Many things happen in cycles. The earth moves in a cycle around the sun and the moon cycles around the earth. The human race moves through a cycle of birth to death, each new generation starting a new cycle. As women, we move through the cycle of our life stages: infancy, puberty (adolescence), sexual maturation (reproductive age), climacteric period (perimenopause and menopause), and post-climacteric (elderly) years.

During the approximate forty years of menstruation, our bodies constantly cycle. We have cycles with our relationships, jobs, and many other areas of our lives. Female sexuality in history also has a cycle, from the ancient times of goddesses such as Aphrodite and her sexuality being worshipped, to more recent times, when women's sexuality was feared and women were locked away, their sexual hysteria surgically cut out of them. This history cycle has taken centuries to occur.

Now, once again society is beginning to see female sexuality as something magnificent; that is to be embraced, respected and welcomed. This time we are not looking towards worshipping at the feet of goddesses - we are finding the sexual sensual goddess we each have within us. We are embracing our sexuality and fitting it into our own interpretation of what that means within our individual lives and beliefs. We can express our sexuality as we see fit, we make our own choices and can refuse to allow something so integral to being a woman, to be defined by other people. You are a goddess, not in a whimsical sense - although we can be playful - but in a way that gives us absolute autonomy for our sexual pleasure and how we choose to express ourselves sexually. Your sexual pleasure is not something that is given to you or permitted by another, it is something that has always been within you and it was always yours to own.

Your inner goddess has always been a part of you, she is you. **You were always a goddess.**

Resources available at www.KazRileyWoman.com

25.   *Reconnection with your Inner Goddess*

It's time to return to your erotic bathtub.

- Imagine removing your clothing and gently submerge yourself in your healing pool. The temperature is exactly right for you. You rest your head, gently supported as your body absorbs the healing, knowledge and acceptance of these powerful waters. You find that you can just let go. Give yourself permission to relax, mentally, emotionally, physically. Nothing to do now, just relaxing.

- As you breathe and as you relax, you become aware of a calm, soothing presence. It is your Inner Goddess - she has always been there and has come to communicate with you.

- Become aware of your Inner Goddess, sense her, maybe you feel her presence as a feeling - notice a colour, some type of light or energy. Perhaps you are aware of her voice. But it doesn't matter how you perceive her, just know that she is there.

- Take this time now to communicate with her, she knows what is in the depths of your heart. Allow her to show you that your sexuality is multi-faceted; you have sexual energy that is powerful and strong, feminine and masculine, fierce and gentle.

- She can show you the way to connect to your powerful yoni (your centre for creation). It is the space in which you birth new life, the space in which your lifeforce feeds the creative and sexual expression is nurtured and accumulates. You are a woman and you are blessed to house these magical powers.

- Your yoni is an entire unique universe of its own. Your healthy yoni has you feeling inspired, sexy and connected to yourself from a very rooted, grounded place. On a very physical level, a healthy yoni has you feeling juicy all over, energised from underneath and smelling delicious.

- Your yoni harnesses so much power and can bring you great pleasure, pleasure that allows you to connect with yourself and your Inner Goddess. Your sacred yoni can release into pleasure to be experienced with others, so that you can be enjoyed, worshipped even, and can fully express and release your intense feminine energy that is rooted and connected to all energy.

- So, as you go deeper now, allow yourself to breathe slowly and deeply, feeling safe as a beautiful light embraces you, filling your body with energy and light.

- Feel your whole body relax. Allow yourself to notice the wonder of your femininity as you direct the light to move through you.

- Notice the light and energy accumulating in your pelvis, your sacred and feminine space that is absorbing the light, letting go of tension, letting go of guilt, of shame, letting go of trauma allowing that wonderful and divine energy to heal.

- You become aware of how completely and wonderfully you are attached and tuned in to your empowering feminine energy and the absolute acceptance of the joy and pleasure it brings. A feeling of self-love, self-pleasure, self-care, as you allow the power to build, not only now but as you move forwards.

- Experience a sense of lightness. Of freedom. Of empowerment. And you know that all shall be well. Any time you wish, you can close your eyes, take a deep breath, commune briefly with your Inner Goddess. She is part of you, she is you.

As we have journeyed together through this book you have come to know that:

- You are capable of experiencing sexual bliss!

- Your sexual energy is a vital part of your happiness and health!

- Your sexual pleasure is multi-layered - mind, body and environment.

- Sexual pleasure is not all about orgasm!

- Your sexual pleasure is unique and individual.

- You are never too old to find your sexual pleasure.

- Your sexual pleasure is your responsibility.

- Eroticism is a crucial part of your sexual pleasure.

- You are a profoundly sensual being.

- Giving yourself permission to receive and experience pleasure is not selfish.

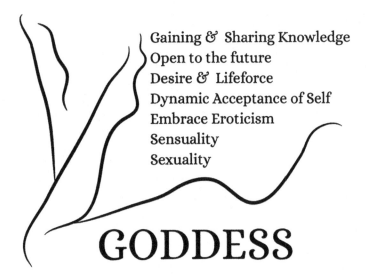

Gaining & Sharing Knowledge
Open to the future
Desire & Lifeforce
Dynamic Acceptance of Self
Embrace Eroticism
Sensuality
Sexuality

GODDESS

You have **gained knowledge and can share that knowledge**, such as how your body works, sexual anatomy, sensuality, and finding your sexual pleasure.

You have changed your mindset and become **open to the future,** a different sexual future by reclaiming your sexual pleasure from shame, your past and the things that were dampening your lifeforce.

You have learned how to feed your own **desire and lifeforce** by embracing your eroticism, having good boundaries, knowing your preferences and listening to your "yes's and no's" and understanding how and when you want to be touched.

You have actively and dynamically **accepted yourself,** your mind, your body, your ability to be sexual, your difficulties, your sensuality and anything else that makes you, you.

You have **embraced your eroticism** and now understand that your inner fantasy world is vital to your sexual pleasure and desire. You have learned the ways your body and mind can be stimulated and eroticised, and that novelty is key to that process.

You have **connected to your sensuality** using all of your senses and can experience the world so that your erotic bathtub is continually filled and overflowing with your vibrant sensual energy, so that your experiences are juicy and fulfilling.

You have **reclaimed and connected to your sexuality,** embracing your sexual pleasure, understanding that is much more than an orgasm, and learned how to *glide* and become fully immersed within it.

As you move forward now, remember that your sexual pleasure needs to be loved and nurtured, that it is a vital part of being a woman. Your sexual pleasure needs your attention. Your sexual pleasure is yours to embrace, and yours to enjoy, on your terms. This is the end of this book, but it is only the start of your journey. Experiment, be playful, explore, fill your erotic bathtub until it overflows and immerse yourself in your sexual pleasure. Be enchanted and enchant others, after all, you are one of the most magnificent creations in the universe -you are a Woman.

About the author

Kaz Riley is an award-winning and leading international clinical hypnotist, sex educator and hypnotherapy trainer. Her work with clients to overcome sexual difficulties has earned her an international reputation for excellence and innovation in the field of sexual freedom therapy, and she received the award hypnotist of the year 2019.

Kaz was the first UK hypnotherapist to be a coalition partner of the National Coalition for sexual freedom in the USA. Kaz's expertise is called upon by international women's and health magazines, podcasts, online health articles, radio, and T.V.

As the creator and founder of sexual freedom hypnosis®, Kaz has trained practitioners worldwide and is a regular speaker at hypnosis and sexual health conventions across the globe. She has also given numerous guest lectures at several U.K. medical, nursing and midwifery schools.

Kaz has a popular sex-positive and hypnosis themed YouTube channel *Trancing in the Sheets*. Kaz passionately believes that everyone should have the ability to choose to have a positive and fulfilling sex life and to be able to easily experience their sexual pleasure and do that in the absence of sexual dysfunction, guilt or shame.

Get in touch

www.kazrileywoman.com

www.sexualfreedomhypnosis.org

Twitter @trancingsheets

Instagram @trancingsheets

Join my Facebook group: www.facebook.com/groups/kazrileywoman

Watch on YouTube

www.youtube.com/c/TrancingintheSheetswithKazRiley

Email: kaz@trancinginthesheets.com

For client seminars and 1:1 therapy sessions with Kaz visit
www.kazrileywoman.com

Sexual freedom training for therapists www.sexualfreedomhypnosis.org